From the River to the Sea

Humanizing Freedom

Reem Borrows

Red Thread Publishing LLC. 2023

Write to **info@redthreadbooks.com** if you are interested in publishing with Red Thread Publishing. Learn more about publications or foreign rights acquisitions of our catalog of books: www.redthreadbooks.com

Paperback ISBN: 978-1-955683-98-2

Ebook ISBN: 978-1-955683-96-8

Cover Design: Red Thread Designs

Cover Photo: VanderWolf Images WesternWall at the Dome of the Rock on the Temple Mount Jerusalem, Israel

Author Headshot: Tommy Collier, DenverHeadshots.com

Contents

Dedication

Division dilutes and is not true.

Like a mother's love,
be authentic and more so be true.

With an open mind and an open heart,
treat others as you would
have them treat you.

- One God
- One Mother Earth
- One Land
- One race: the human race
- One Love
- One Dream

Forewords

We are grateful to have a couple forewords offered for this book representing various voices.

~

As Saint Paul famously said: we human beings "see through a glass darkly." Our focus is shaped by experience, by the narratives that have formed us, by partisan and at times prejudicial influences that have surrounded us, and most of all we "see" through the fears we cling to.

This book will help us see with greater clarity the pathway that must be taken to peaceful coexistence out of the current morass of violence in the lands of the Holy One. As some read the title of this remarkable book they might see in it a claim by Palestinians, or by Israelis, for complete and exclusive sovereignty of this "Holy Land." Such has become the mantra of those who seek domination over others.

This would be a terrible misreading of the title, and a misunderstanding of its use by Reem Borrows and others who seek universal and common equity for all who live between the river and the sea. The author is clear that no one can own or have sovereignty over these lands. The lands own the people who reside in them, requiring connectivity with the landscape, respect for all whose sandals have traversed every hill and wadi, and reverence for ancestors who call to them from every synagogue, mosque, church, and sacred sites.

Borrows is an Australian Christian Palestinian, born in Haifa, with a large extended family living in and around this historic city. She is in a unique position to convey a Palestinian perspective in a manner accessible to Western ears that, consciously or not, are generally conditioned to hear only an Israeli narrative. This partisan positioning has, for too long, enjoyed Western political and media favor, if not, seemingly, Divine imprimatur.

The book contains historical and cultural information which is important to grasp in understanding the context of the terrible events of October 7, 2023 and its violent aftermath. This book makes it clear that such extreme violence can never serve the cause of peace; indeed, retributive violence makes further violence inevitable.

However, of greater significance than times, dates, and places, are the themes she pursues. The themes are important for a greater understanding of the Palestine/Israel situation, but they are also important in the understanding of all our contexts. The Israel/Palestine struggle illustrates human failures and vulnerabilities common to us all. Connectivity is a major theme. These lands will never experience the peace they long for while the vulnerable are oppressed and excluded by the powerful. These lands and its peoples are like shards of an earthenware pot eroding beside each other, longing for reassembly by a master craftsman. Borrows makes it clear this craftsman is not a single person, but Palestinian and Jewish peoples who share a common vision lived out in respect, dignity and honor across the boundaries that currently divide.

Victimhood is another significant theme. That Jews have been victims of historical prejudice culminating in the Holocaust is a shameful fact of history. It is equally true that Palestinians have been victims of a never-ending Nakba since 1948. However, seeking power and advantage through victimhood blights any prospect for peace and well-being.

Yet another theme is the use of fear by the powerful as they seek to hold on to power. We do not need the Middle East to introduce us to this theme. We are very alert to the reality that politicians in democracies, as much as dictatorships, use fear as a primary tool in obtaining power and subsequently exercising influence. As Borrows articulates this theme, we are led into a deeper understanding of fear being the opposite of love.

Borrows's Christian identity specifically challenges those who seek to categorize the Israeli/Palestinian struggle as a window into a broader conflict between Islamic extremism and Western values, as it is not a religious struggle.

This book should be read by all who seek a genuine understanding of the struggle for common and equal humanity and of the direction a pathway for peace and goodwill for Palestinians and Israelis alike must take.

It has been an honor to be invited to write the Foreword.

The Right Reverend Doctor George Browning
    Retired Anglican Bishop of Canberra Goulburn
    President Australia Palestine Advocacy Network 2013–2022

From the River to the Sea is a timely and important intervention into the sadness and devastation we have witnessed historically and most recently in the Holy Land.

"This land doesn't belong to any of us; we belong to her."

The Holy Land yearns for her children, all of them, Jew, Christian and Muslim; she is the thread that binds all of the children of Abraham. It is only in embracing this thread and accepting that our collective peace is assured when we live as one, together, in equality that we and the land will know peace.

Exclusivist ideologies of superiority must be challenged with the language of inclusion and belonging.

It is only with this spirit of love, compassion and sharing that peace can be achieved.

For, in the end, none of us is free unless all of us are free.

Nasser Mashni,
    President of Australia Palestine Advocacy Network (APAN)
    and founding board member of Olive Kids

Introduction

This is not the book I set out to write, yet this is the book that needed to be born.

The book I was writing was initially intended to explore the intricacies of leadership in individuals, teams, and organizations of all sizes. As a long-time leadership consultant, I was sharing what I teach my clients around the world. However, as I delved into the subject, I realized that there was another narrative needing my immediate attention—one of the worst humanitarian crises of our time that relates to leadership on a global level.

The crisis I speak of is not just an isolated incident but a symptom of a deeper and ongoing failure we, as humans, are actively perpetuating. This is why *From the River to the Sea: Humanizing Freedom* became my primary focus— to shed light on the underlying flaws responsible for our current predicament, with the present tragedy being the most urgent but certainly not the last if we persist on our current trajectory. While finalizing and publishing this book the situation has only gotten worse, with the whole world witnessing.

In this exploration, I found myself uniquely positioned to address the issue. Born a Palestinian-Christian with Israeli Citizenship, I grew up in a world that deemed me a second-class citizen. Yet my family had some opportunities that created possibilities for us: my parents were studying in England where we were exposed to being judged on merit. For the first time, we experienced the freedom to be treated on equal terms. This perspective, coupled with our immigration to Australia, where warmth and welcome greeted us as soon as we landed in Sydney, are critical moments that shaped my understanding of true freedom. The customs officer in Sydney met us with understanding and a warm welcome. Our Palestinian identity was not an instant condemnation; we were seen as equals for the first time. This contrast has been etched in my memory—an Australia that embraced us for who we are with no judgement, as opposed to in our own country where we had faced discrimination. That moment marked my introduction to true freedom.

I've been fortunate to experience the true essence of freedom—a freedom that rises above ethnic and religious divides. Here, in Australia, I've found a safe home where judgement is reserved for the merit of my hard work, values, and contributions, allowing me to experience all of life's joys without prejudice and fear.

My passion has led me to study with a Buddhist Monk and talk to rabbis and priests, as well as renowned thought leaders like Bob Proctor and Neale Donald Walsch. I have been mentored by some of the best CEOs, and have been part of Global Business Leadership Pathways in Korea, as well as the NAU PEAK Program Flagship of the Accelerated Development Program for Novartis Asia/Harvard University in Shanghai. I am a graduate of the Australian Institute of Company Directors. I have woven my studies, formal and informal, with my life and business experience and presented a perspective to serve the world.

This book unfolds in two sections: The first delves into the events of the past and present, employing logic and facts to understand the root cause of the crisis from an intellectual perspective with references added. The second section is a heartfelt call to action, urging readers to tap into their feeling selves. I sprinkle historical and personal stories throughout where relevant to guide and illuminate. In a world that now, more than ever, needs a collective shift towards operating from the heart, we should be using our minds as intelligent servants rather than allowing them to create chaos and destruction.

This book aligns with my expertise as an executive coach and business consultant, where I specialize in leadership. The principles rooted in the *Dreem Health, Head, and Heart Leadership framework,* initially meant for individuals, teams, and organizations, find broader application in the global geopolitical situation. You will find at times I quote thought leaders, political leaders, and spiritual leaders then delve into the mechanics of the mind, personal development, as well as teachings from different faiths. It may seem strange at first to be bringing all these elements together but I have spent many years with different mentors learning and applying the principles of leadership, organizational psychology, connective spiritualism, and the universal laws that govern our every creation. Everything is connected, and the concepts I share have been written about for thousands of years. This book is not only a call to address the urgent crisis but also a call for nations to recognize that developing "whole" leaders globally and at all levels is paramount.

This book goes beyond crisis and critique; it's a guide toward a transformative leadership that displays "Grace Under Pressure," as articulated by Ernest Hemingway—a leadership that acknowledges both the head and the heart as essential elements in navigating the complexities of our interconnected world.

Ultimately, it's an invitation for you as a reader to join me in reexamining how we think, believe, and behave as individuals, organizations, and nations. Together, we have the opportunity to choose a different path—one of love, understanding, and the active honoring and humanization of freedom for all. It is a call to action for current leaders to change how they both think and behave, but also for individuals to adopt a fresh perspective. This is not a matter for only the people in high leadership roles, but on a global scale, we can shift the trajectory of the future together.

Please understand that I never intended this book to be written from a political point of view, as I have no real interest in politics. Though as soon as you mention the word Palestine or Israel, you can be automatically seen as being political. The game of politics is only designed to show people what political parties want to show them, through a narrow lens, to fulfill the party's agenda at any cost through the creation of fear. Politics, like mainstream media, can twist facts and only show snippets of information needed to scare and control people. That is the general modus operandi that we tend to see in politics. I am neither a historian nor an academic, but history generally tends to show the whole picture, and over time, we come to learn the truth. When we open our eyes and learn the truth, we are shocked and can't believe how easily people are deceived, which prompts us to ask ourselves, "How could we have allowed this to happen?"

THE DONKEY, THE TIGER, AND THE LION

> *The donkey told the tiger, "The grass is blue."*
> *The tiger replied, "No, the grass is green."*
> *The discussion became heated and the two decided to submit the issue to arbitration, so they approached the lion.*
> *As they approached the lion on his throne, the donkey started screaming: "Your Highness, isn't it true that the grass is blue?"*
> *The lion replied: "If you believe it is true, then the grass is blue."*
> *The donkey rushed forward and continued, "The tiger disagrees with me, contradicts me, and annoys me. Please punish him."*

*Then the king declared, "The tiger will be punished
with 3 days of silence."
The donkey jumped with joy and went on his way,
content and repeating, "The grass is blue. The
grass is blue..."
The tiger asked the lion, "Your Majesty, why have you
punished me, after all, the grass is green?"
The lion replied, "You've known and seen the grass is
green."
The tiger asked, "So, why do you punish me?"
The lion replied, "That has nothing to do with the
question of whether the grass is blue or green.
The punishment is that it is degrading for a brave,
intelligent creature like you to waste time arguing
with an ass, and on top of that, you came and both-
ered me with that question just to validate something you already knew was true!"*

∾

This story reminds me that the biggest waste of time is arguing with a
fool and fanatic who doesn't care about truth or reality, but only the
victory of his/her beliefs and illusions. Never waste time on discus-
sions that make no sense.

There are people who, for all the evidence presented to them,
cannot understand what has been laid bare before them. Others are
blinded by ego, hatred, and resentment and the only thing that they
want is to be right, even if they aren't.

When IGNORANCE SCREAMS, intelligence moves on.

"Speak not in the ears of a fool: for he will despise the wisdom of thy
words."

— Proverbs 23:9 KJV

It is easy to forget, but don't worry about the donkeys you encounter in life. Find the other tigers and lions.[1]

How Change is Made

To mobilize change and bring it to fruition, you need critical mass. Over the centuries, we have seen so many shifts, which have triggered us to evolve in our beliefs, attitudes, and legislation in many areas of society. We once believed the earth was flat. Opposing the Church's views was punishable by death, and women were burnt at the stake. Women also had no rights to vote, work, or have their own bank accounts. Same-sex marriage was unheard of and such liaisons were also punishable by death. Interracial marriage was illegal, and slavery was commonplace and justified. Even South African apartheid was not only tolerated, but it was also supported by many nations for a time.

Colonization and the abuse of the Indigenous populations were seen as "the civilized thing to do." In Australia, we had a government policy that resulted in what is now known as the "Stolen Generation," which took place between the early 1900s and the 1970s. Young Indigenous children were ripped out of their mothers' arms, removed from their families, and taken to over 480 institutions where they were put into foster care and adoption to learn the "white people's ways" and denied the right to speak their language or practice their own culture.[2] These children were often subjected to abuse. The impact this has had on them, their families, and the subsequent generations has been horrific. It's a similar story for the Indigenous people in Canada, the United States, and many other colonized lands.

It makes you shudder to think of what was allowed to happen and accepted in our recent history, and it's hard to fathom how people held these views. To add salt to the wound, the facts were denied, hidden, and even turned around to make the victims look like the bad guys. At the time though, people truly believed they were doing the right thing and could justify their actions. Even to this day, people who have never experienced such atrocity, or studied history objectively, wonder why those impacted "can't just get on with it" and assimilate; they can't understand why there needs to be an acknowledgment and an apology to move on, to heal, and to rebuild.

Considering these occurrences, we still have a long way to go, and in recent years, especially since the COVID pandemic, it feels like the division has grown and we have taken a few steps backward. If you feel like we still have much work to do globally, you may not be wrong.

Yet, we can't deny what was once believed to be true has, over time, changed in many parts of the world, and we have seen some real shifts. As humans though, it often feels like we are slow to learn and we should be doing so much more given that we are in the year 2023. However, that is all relative, isn't it?

Take a Wider View

We view history as being a few thousand years old since we started to write, or we see it as being a few million years old and dinosaurs being long-term history. Yet, that does not in any way compare to the real history of our universe. Human history in the grand scheme of things plays only a minuscule role in the whole picture. Even the time of dinosaurs in recent history relative to the universal timeline plays only a small part. It can be hard to fathom the real concept of time and where we sit concerning this. Carl Sagan (1934–1996) helped us understand the real significance and contribution of humans to date in comparison to the total history of our universe. To give us an idea of relativity, he graphically illustrated the history of the universe by compressing it into one year and showing us the relativity of events over 13.7 billion years.[3]

At the time scale of a revised cosmic calendar:

1 year = 13.7 billion years
1 month = 1.1 billion years
1 day = 37.5 million years
1 hour = 1.5 million years
1 minute = 26,000 years
1 second = 434 years
0.16 seconds = 1 modern human lifetime

Source: https://en.wikipedia.org/wiki/Cosmic_Calendar

Our planet has existed for approximately 4.5 billion years,[4] which equates to just under four hours in Sagan's Cosmic Calendar. The earliest record of people in Australia was only 65,000 years ago, equating to 2.5 minutes, while colonization of the Americas, India, and Australia was roughly 320 years ago. World War 1, dubbed the "war to end all wars," was only 108 years ago. The atomic bombs were dropped by the U.S. on Hiroshima and Nagasaki, and genocide became a crime under international law about seventy-seven years ago. The first astronaut set foot on the moon fifty-three years ago. Amazon Online was launched twenty-nine years ago, being the largest cloud-based platform. Then we saw the worldwide adoption of the Declaration on the Rights of Indigenous Peoples approximately sixteen years ago. Two-thirds of the world's population only gained access to safe drinking water about twelve years before the writing of this book.

Now, can you see how relative to the universe and our planet's existence, we are still very immature and like "babes in the woods"? Yes, as a species, we have many self-destructive tendencies; however, we have seen changes over a short period for the betterment of humanity. If we look at the big picture and timeline, we will find that we have barely begun, and we are continuing to learn so much. Our history equating to a mere 0.16 seconds on the cosmic calendar puts things into perspective. The challenge for most of us is we expect everything to be solved now and, in our lifetime, given that we tend to think of it as being a very long time. But it's not. If we put things in perspective, however, slow down, and reflect, then perhaps we will be able to solve all the so-called challenges that have been caused as a result of our self-destructive ways. Then we can evolve and mature to improve the quality of our existence globally.

Let us work together to extend a ray of hope in these dark times. There is always a reason to despair, just as there is to celebrate; where we choose to put our focus creates our experience of the world. Let's open our hearts and minds to the possibility that peace is achievable and explore how we can accomplish this together.

Addendum

A Call for Peace and Justice in the Face of Recent Tragedy

In Gaza's tear-stained skies, a desperate plea,
Palestinians suffer, hearts in agony.
A world looks on, their dignity undone,
Why do we hesitate to aid each one?

Is it their lack of arms, their meager purse,
That leaves them in this never-ending curse?
Or is it innocence, their shield and plight,
That keeps their cries from reaching day and night?

When Jesus, filled with anguish and despair,
Gazed heavenward, in sorrow-laden prayer,
He spoke not just as God but as a man,
Who understood humanity's cruel plan.

"Forgive them, Father," were his words of grace,
Not from divine heights, but in an earthly place,
As Jesus knew, only salvation from above,
Could heal the wounds and mend the bonds of love.

Let Gaza's plight, in all its tragic throes,
Remind us of compassion that still grows.
For in our hearts, the power to empathize,
Can spark a change that opens tear-filled eyes.

The pain of Gaza, Palestine's deep sigh,
Should make us all question, "What if that were I?"
Let love and justice be our guiding call,
To halt the spreading darkness that befalls us all.

In Gaza's name, let empathy take wing,
For every life, let dignity and peace we bring.
May God forgive us for our silent cries,
And unite us all beneath compassionate skies.

It is with a heavy heart and deep sorrow that I find myself revisiting my book *From the River to the Sea* in light of the deeply distressing events that unfolded in Gaza after the attacks on the 7th of October 2023.

Just two weeks prior, I signed a contract for the publication of this book, which I believed could contribute to helping people understand the situation and how we could achieve peace and justice on equal terms.

I want to make it unequivocally clear that I do not condone any form of violence, and I view the recent events with a sense of immense sadness and knowledge that this situation could escalate quickly to becoming a horrific catastrophe beyond what the world has seen so far.

In the aftermath of the Gaza breakout and the tragic loss of innocent lives, the Israeli government announced its decision to sever essential services, including electricity, water, and gas, from Gaza. Israel, with backing from the United States of America, with alarming speed, deployed its forces in a manner that bore the hallmarks of a carpet-bombing and ethnic-cleansing exercise.

Reports from doctors and civilians on the ground paint an ugly picture: Gaza, home to over 2.3 million people, stands on the cliff of a humanitarian catastrophe. The despair felt is beyond words.

This moment signifies just the beginning of a larger plan of destruction unless we, as a global community, act swiftly and decisively to put an end to this cycle. A simple post I shared on Facebook, "God forgive us all," reflects the despair and helplessness I felt at the time. This made me think of the moment when Jesus, the man, in the depths of his own agony, asked his Father to "Forgive them."

When I wrote the post, I had a sudden realization that his plea was not an expression of an all-forgiving benevolence; rather, it stemmed from the recognition of our human weaknesses and vulnerability. Jesus realized we are too often led by fear, blinded by false narratives, and, regrettably, willing to turn a blind eye to oppression and brutality. He looked up to his Father and asked for forgiveness in pure despair.

When will we understand that we are all interconnected and the current aggression will only fuel further suffering? When will we understand that violence begets violence, and it will persist until we address its roots? When will we realize that we need to act now to prevent a future where we ask why similar atrocities are happening to us?

God forgive us all, and may we find the strength to walk the path towards lasting peace, justice, and compassion for all.

My book, *From the River to the Sea*, now feels very mild-mannered and optimistic in this moment of crisis. My heart is heavy with despair and sorrow. I am torn between these emotions and have a need to urge people to wake up from the haze of false media perspectives and social media narratives. This crisis is not isolated; it's part of a broader pattern that we have to confront. Despite the pain being felt by Palestinians, they will never consider themselves to be victims or play that role, nor will they succumb to oppression, land theft, colonization, and brutality.

The world is witnessing a shocking reality as the war in Gaza enters its second week, with a devastating toll—which is growing fast —of over 8,000 lives lost, half of them innocent children. The minute-by-minute updates of the ongoing destruction and loss are deeply distressing. The decimation of essential infrastructure, including churches, hospitals, and safe havens, reflects the severity of the situation. Tragically, deliberate attacks on journalists have aimed to stifle the flow of information to the world.

Globally, a rapid surge of peaceful public demonstrations have emerged. London saw a staggering turnout of 500,000 individuals demanding a ceasefire, while in New York, groups like Jewish Voice for Peace-New York City, halted Grand Central Station. This, too, is growing. Never before in my lifetime have I witnessed such widespread public support and the display of so many Palestinian flags.

While the United States, Canada, and Australia have yet to take decisive action to demand a ceasefire, public pressure is intensifying, fostering rapidly increasing momentum. Extremist views persist on both sides, but the prevailing moderate majority is gaining momentum, indicating the critical mass outlined in early parts of my book.

At this critical stage, there is a hopeful belief, perhaps even a prayer, that this catastrophic event could ultimately be the catalyst to pave the way for peace and justice in the region for all. It's unfortunate that the situation had to deteriorate to such an extent before significant strides toward resolution can be made. I am often baffled by human behavior and ask myself why do things have to get so bad before they get better? But I guess that is just part of our human condition as an immature species.

I'm deeply troubled by the global perception of powerful governments that this war is righteous and justifiable, allowing the occupying force to defend itself with such excessive force. While we ask for the safe return of the hostages, there's a disconcerting notion that the Israeli government might not prioritize their release, potentially sacrificing them. Whether this is true or not remains to be seen.

I can't help but reflect on how easily people are swayed by propaganda and led into a narrative of hate and division. Throughout history, every genocide has been rationalised by its leaders. At the time, these actions never seemed inherently evil; the grim reality only became apparent in the aftermath. They were often portrayed as patriotic, justifiable, and much needed, but such appalling events never occurred without some level of support. Even silence becomes complicity in the unfolding tragedy.

There is a documented process which infiltrates the subconscious mind, that can dampen our innate compassion. It involves these main steps:

- Fostering fear to activate survival instincts.
- Stripping the "other" of their humanity through dehumanization.
- Applying broad generalizations to a select few, portraying them as faceless targets deserving of destruction

This manipulation aims to desensitize us, destroying the foundations of our humanity. But there is a way out of this, which is our sole hope for peace and the survival of our species. This can only be done once we set aside prejudices or stereotypes and reconnect with our heart and humanity.

We need to recognize every person is not just a number; each person has their own dreams and aspirations, and they are loved by family members. True peace doesn't reside in war but rather within each of us, and in our voices. So now, more than ever, each one of us has to speak up. Rekindling empathy and humanity gives us the power to alter this dangerous narrative and path we are traveling on. Our collective voice and shared humanity will forge the way for a future of peace and harmony. Each one of us has the ability to make a difference.

This recent escalation of violence and destruction makes you realize the urgent need to say "Enough is enough." The key lies in understanding that everyone involved, even those observing from a distance and staying quiet, faces immense loss. The people of Gaza, left with nothing and with nowhere to go, have felt the brunt for far too long. If this cycle persists, the devastation will spread and intensify.

This land doesn't belong to any of us; we belong to her. It's time to end apartheid, occupation, division, and brutality. The land from the river to the sea is home to us all, and we don't need more suffering. I urge anyone who is taking sides with no thought of the other to reconsider and stand for the only true side—Peace and Justice on Equal Terms.

To the international community, this is a call to open your eyes and put an end to this complacency and one-sided view of the issue.

The core points of my book *From the River to the Sea* are timeless. We must end apartheid, military occupation, and privileges granted to one people over another, and work with a new model based on a solution with no divisions and equal rights for all, which includes the right of return for all Palestinians in the exact same way as their Jewish counterparts. It's either freedom for all, or freedom for none.

The events in Gaza are a wake-up call and a reminder of the urgency of these issues.

The time for change is now, and it is my hope and dream that through understanding, empathy, and a shared vision of peace, we can put an end to this unnecessary madness to welcome coexistence and harmony.

Justice and freedom for all are my final words.

In solidarity and with a heavy heart,
    Reem Borrows
    (October 2023)

Timeline

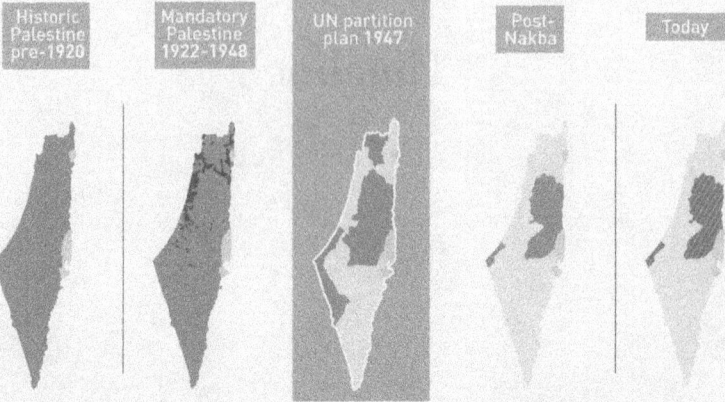

What is Nakba?

Nakba (Arabic for 'catastrophe') refers to the ethnic cleansing of Palestine in 1948 by Zionist militias to make way for the creation of Israel.

Palestine
Jewish-owned land
Israel
Israeli-occupied

Historic Palestine pre-1920

Mandatory Palestine 1922-1948

UN partition plan 1947

Post-Nakba

Today

M≡E
middleeasteye.net

Source https://www.palestineportal.org/learn-teach/israelpalestine-the-basics/maps/maps-loss-of-land/

Nakba: A Timeline

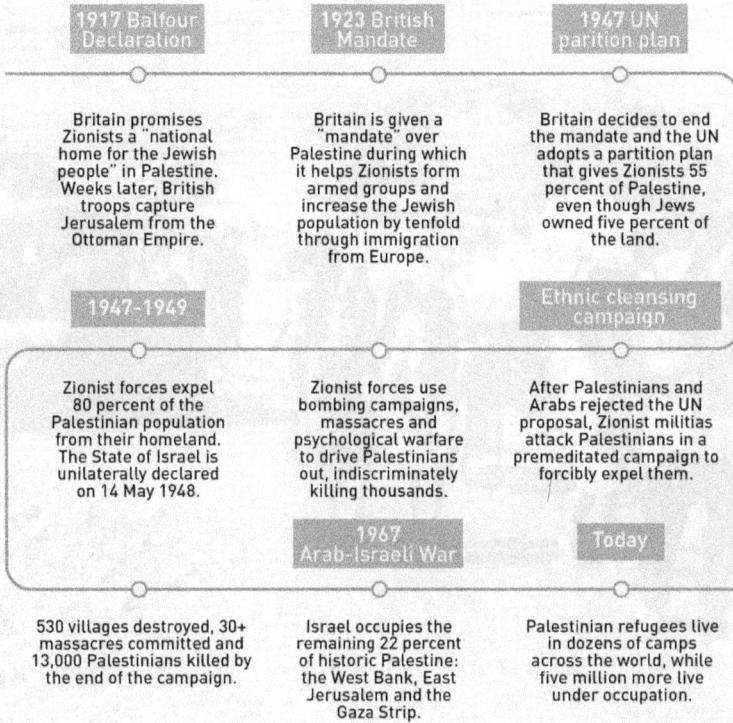

1917 Balfour Declaration

Britain promises Zionists a "national home for the Jewish people" in Palestine. Weeks later, British troops capture Jerusalem from the Ottoman Empire.

1923 British Mandate

Britain is given a "mandate" over Palestine during which it helps Zionists form armed groups and increase the Jewish population by tenfold through immigration from Europe.

1947 UN parition plan

Britain decides to end the mandate and the UN adopts a partition plan that gives Zionists 55 percent of Palestine, even though Jews owned five percent of the land.

1947-1949

Zionist forces expel 80 percent of the Palestinian population from their homeland. The State of Israel is unilaterally declared on 14 May 1948.

Zionist forces use bombing campaigns, massacres and psychological warfare to drive Palestinians out, indiscriminately killing thousands.

Ethnic cleansing campaign

After Palestinians and Arabs rejected the UN proposal, Zionist militias attack Palestinians in a premeditated campaign to forcibly expel them.

530 villages destroyed, 30+ massacres committed and 13,000 Palestinians killed by the end of the campaign.

1967 Arab-Israeli War

Israel occupies the remaining 22 percent of historic Palestine: the West Bank, East Jerusalem and the Gaza Strip.

Today

Palestinian refugees live in dozens of camps across the world, while five million more live under occupation.

Source https://www.middleeasteye.net/news/israel-palestine-nakba-ethnic-cleansing-explained-five-maps-charts

Part One

The Head

Chapter 1

CHILD OF PEACE

As We All Are Born

To this day, tension experienced in Palestine in 2021 across the whole country continues to grow at an alarming rate. The bombings were relentless, the drones flying over Gaza were loud, and the raids on homes in the West Bank were escalating, as were the Palestinian protests. Meanwhile, mobs in the northern part of the state were marking the homes of Arabs to identify who would be attacked. The news coverage globally portrayed a crisis at breaking point.

This is not the first time we have seen such an event unfold. However, the difference this time was that the Palestinian protests were happening across the entire country in every sector, and in unity like never before. To many outsiders, it felt like there was no solution.

Peace is Possible

Medical staff at hospitals across the country came together in solidarity to call for peaceful coexistence and cooperation between Jewish and Arab medical personnel during these terrifying times.

Staff at Sheba Medical Center in Tel Hashomer, Rambam Medical
Center in Haifa, Galilee Medical Center in Nahariya, and Emek
Medical Center in Afula all rejected the division and actively
promoted unity.[1] They refused to take part in the violence, division,
and hatred. They were a symbol of, and a model for respect, coexistence, and harmony. Their teams represented all denominations and
beliefs—and their patients came from all over the country with some
from other parts of the Middle East.

Throughout the years, this harmony has existed and stood against
oppression and conflict as a matter of policy. Rambam Hospital in
Haifa, for example, worked to bring people and hearts together.

Rambam General Director, Dr. Michael Halberthal sent the
following email to all hospital team members, calling to protect the
special place that Rambam has built over the years:

"Dear Rambam Employees,

*We are all witnessing the recent events in the country, which are
characterized by great tension and violence. Rambam is a hospital
where members of all denominations and religions from all walks of
life work side by side. We are all united around only one goal—to help
our patients recover and make their hospitalizations easier.*

*Each of us holds diverse personal opinions and worldviews, but
all of these are irrelevant to our shared mission in the hospital.*

*I hope and believe that Rambam, as a family with differences,
will remain an island of sanity within the uneasy reality around us,
standing together as we have done during all of the difficult trials we
have experienced in recent years.*

*Therefore, when we, the employees from all the different sectors,
enter the hospital and put on our work clothes, we leave the turbulent
world behind us and concentrate on our shared goals.*

*We have built a special 'home' here, one that we nurture as a
place of harmony and inclusivity. One of which I am personally
proud to be a part of. Let us keep it going together.*

With profound appreciation,

Michael Halberthal
General Director[2]

Rambam Health Care Campus employees chose to convey a strong message to all, stating that "we are together." The medical staff, nursing staff, and employees throughout the hospital showed unity, peace, coexistence, and solidarity, with many of them taking part in a campaign demonstrating how colleagues and friends from different religions work side by side to provide the best possible healthcare. They were photographed together, carrying signs of peace to demonstrate their strong stance.

Rambam's Arab and Jewish doctors, nurses, paramedics, and other team members held rallies, with an unambiguous slogan, "Jews and Arabs refuse to be enemies." The organizers—Professor Gil Bolotin, Director of the Department of Cardiac Surgery; Professor Mogher Khamaisi, Director of the Department of Internal Medicine and Dr. Diab Mutlek, an attending physician in the Non-invasive Cardiology Unit—said, "We work side by side in the departments and the operating rooms. We are one big family, and this is our message."

Unfortunately, we did not see much media coverage, neither locally nor globally, describing this unity and the potential we have for peace on equal terms and coexistence void of borders and division. When you learn of these movements, however, you quickly realize what is possible. A clearly defined goal that all team members strive towards can break down all walls and hatred. If we can experience this in hospitals, where else can we create this? Our potential is huge.

My Story

I'll always look back at my childhood as being a beautiful one with the warmest of memories. It's hard for me to even fault my childhood as I was surrounded by a huge extended family that was full of fun, unconditional love, and support. Anywhere I went in the old country, I had my immediate and extended family ties to count on. From city to city, village to village, I was surrounded by an incredible abundance of joy, love, and genuine hospitality. I had a huge sense of belonging and a deep inner feeling of pure love.

When I look back and reflect on these feelings, my heart warms and I am amazed at how strong these feelings were, despite growing up in a system that supported religious and ethnic segregation. A system that differentiated one group of people over another group who had lived on the land for centuries.

You see, I am a Palestinian Christian born in the city of Haifa on the Mediterranean shore. I am proud to say I was born in Rambam Hospital. My family is from the Galilee region, Jesus Christ's hometown, and we are descendants of the first Christians in the world. My mother, grandmother and maternal great-grandmother were all born in Palestine, with a lineage you can follow back.

Like the first Christians from the Galilee region, the streets of Haifa and Nazareth were my playground. My family lived in the old parts of the cities, where Jesus lived and played as a child and walked through as a man. There he taught people how to love, stood up to and fought injustice, questioned the hierarchy, questioned the division as well as rejected the separation of one people from another based on faith, status, ethnicity, and wealth. In my neighborhood, he started a global movement based on pure love and oneness.

I was born in the same area as my ancestors but by then—and due to the "Nakba" (the catastrophe) in 1948—we were no longer allowed to call ourselves Palestinian. In Arabic, "Nakba" refers to the mass expulsion of Palestinians in 1948 during the creation of Israel. We lived as second-class citizens at best, under a new political regime that did not recognize our people's history or their right to be there. In 1948 and again in 1967, most Palestinians lost their lands, homes, titles, and deeds, if not their lives.

To this day, there is a Palestinian refugee crisis. As of 2019, more than 5.6 million Palestinians were registered with UNRWA as refugees. The term "Palestinian refugee" does not include internally displaced Palestinians. The Palestinians living as refugees are scattered all over the Middle East with no papers, no rights, no freedom, no real recognition, and—if that isn't enough—with no right to return to their birthplace and home!

Today, the State of Israel has been recognized by several organizations as an Apartheid Regime. Amnesty International 2022 declared, "the Israeli government is committing the crime against humanity of apartheid against Palestinians and must be held accountable," after releasing its nearly 280-page report.

The Israeli Information Center for Human Rights in the Occupied Territories (B'Tselem) also declared Israel as an Apartheid State. Since B'Tselem's inception in 1989, they documented, researched, and published statistics, testimonies, video footage, position papers, and reports on human rights violations committed by Israel in the Occupied Territories. According to B'Tselem, "The initial mandate we took upon ourselves focused on the occupation regime in the West Bank (including East Jerusalem) and in the Gaza Strip. However, over the years, it has become clear that the concept of two parallel regimes operating between the Mediterranean Sea and Jordan River—a permanent democracy west of the Green Line and a temporary military occupation to the east of it—is divorced from reality. The entire area under Israeli control is ruled by a single apartheid regime, governing the lives of all people living in it and operating according to one organizing principle: establishing and perpetuating the control of one group of people—Jews—over another—Palestinians—through laws, practices, and state violence."

B'Tselem's mission is to "strive for a future in which human rights, liberty, and equality are guaranteed to all people, Palestinian and Jewish alike, living between the Jordan River and the Mediterranean Sea."

How Could We Have Allowed This to Happen Here and Elsewhere?

Here are some modern-day examples that come to mind. Until recently, many people in Australia had no real comprehension of what our Indigenous community had to endure at the hands of the colonizer. British colonization and subsequent Australian land laws were established on the claim that Australia was *terra nullius*, in other words, "nobody's land." At first contact, there were over 250,000 Aborigines in Australia. The massacres ended in the 1920s, leaving no more than 60,000 Indigenous people.

David Michael Smith from the University of Houston presented a paper called, "Counting the Dead: Estimating the Loss of Life in the Indigenous Holocaust, 1492–Present." It is claimed that "at the turn of the twentieth century, the total number of Native inhabitants living in the entire Western Hemisphere had declined to 4-4.5 million. In 1800, only about 600,000 Indigenous people remained in the United States. By 1900, the Indigenous population in this country reached its lowest point of about 237,000 people..."[3]

How many of us are aware of these facts and how many of us watched the glorified "country and Western movies that depicted the Indigenous community as savages?" How much of this information was taught at schools and acknowledged until recently? History eventually, in most cases, tells us the truth about events. We can look back at history to learn from it. Unfortunately, to date, we seem to keep repeating the same mistakes, but again, we are still very immature as a species and have a lot to learn.

The intention here is to set the scene so as to better understand what is being dealt with, in order to grasp the situation from a perspective that may differ from what has been known so far. Knowledge precedes understanding, which precedes solutions, which can eventually lead to peace on equal terms through coexistence.

Chapter 2

THE AWAKENING

No Longer Justifying Genocide

At one point, we thought it was perfectly reasonable to have slaves, and apartheid was accepted. However, to the vast majority of people today, it defies logic as to how this could have been so. To have made changes such as recognizing Indigenous rights, women's rights, same-sex rights, education rights, and other human rights, to see the end of South Africa's apartheid regime, we needed to become aware of what was actually occurring. We had to become aware of the truth. So, what changed? Well, awareness and critical mass are what happened. It started with only a few people, and over time, it gathered momentum and support to a point where critical mass could influence real change.

In the last few years, it does feel that things may have taken a turn for the worse, globally. We have had the pandemic and its crippling effects on mental health and the global economy, leading us into recession, and potentially, worse. As of 2022 and according to the UNHCR, the number of people who have been forcibly displaced has reached 100 million in total.[1] With economic hardship comes ugly politics, and we are starting to see fearmongering and divisive tactics on the rise again. With so many countries having access to nuclear weapons, people worry as they watch the news, news which is geared to spread even more fear, which, in turn, leaves its audience wondering if it is too late to save our world.

We watch the news and, without much actual understanding of what is going on, we make up our minds as to who the "bad guy" is, and who the "good guy" is. If we are not vigilant in how we think, when we listen to a message enough times, our subconscious mind will start to believe it as truth.

If you are sitting in America, Australia, or England right now, for example, chances are you see Russia as the enemy and Ukraine as the innocent party and victim. Who can blame you, given the type of news and movies over the years you have been bombarded with? But have you ever stopped to question what events in the past 20 years or more have brought us to this point with the Russia/Ukraine situation? And to be very clear, this is not about condoning Putin's actions in any way. It is merely about observing past events that led us to this one. Another event in the news right now is the Israeli-Palestinian conflict. And I use the word "conflict" very loosely. More on this later.

A History of Spin

Have you ever really looked at the events in the past one hundred years to ask yourself, "What is going on in the Holy Land?" Maybe you have watched movies where the perpetrator of a damaging attack or vicious crime is of Arab descent, a Muslim, or something similar, and now you, perhaps inadvertently, associate all Arabs as being "Muslim terrorists." You can liken it to the Hollywood style of movie where an American/Western Soldier is called into an operation to rescue victims from a Muslim siege or attack. Such movies are usually set in Iraq, Syria, Afghanistan, Turkey, Jordan, Lebanon, or Palestine. Is it art imitating life or the other way around? The picture can get blurry.

For a long time, the U.S. government targeted Iraq and Saddam Hussain in an aggressive media campaign, and mainstream media picked it up, hook, line and sinker. The goal of the Iraq war was to destabilize and bring down Saddam Hussain by claiming he had "weapons of mass destruction" and he was harboring Al Qaeda terrorists. It was a media PR strategy of modern times resulting in the death of reportedly over a million Iraqis and the destruction of a whole nation, and these devastating effects are still felt today. No weapons of mass destruction were ever found, and Saddam was removed from power, leaving a country weak and on its knees, allowing for organized extremist groups to create havoc in and around the country, which can still be felt today.[2] Since then, many Hollywood movies have been made on Iraq and we have to ask ourselves what impact such visual storytelling has on our psyche, and is it in any way altering our truth?

Similarly, on mainstream Western media feeds, we regularly hear about Palestinians being terrorists, Muslims wanting a Jihad, and how Israel is just trying to defend itself. But when you consider digging a little deeper, could there be more to the story than what is being told? Maybe you have listened to one particular news channel such as Fox News or CNN, which have their specific agenda, and thought: *This has been going on for thousands of years; it will never be resolved. Besides, it's happening in a distant land, what impact could it possibly have on me?*

Therein lies the biggest challenge we face globally today. We have not yet come to accept that whatever is happening in one place to one person will have an impact on our own lives.

Everything is connected. No event is mutually exclusive from another event. It's like the domino effect. Once the first domino falls, it will impact every other domino thereafter. Individually and globally, we are connected economically (including corporations), politically, and spiritually. The quicker we become aware of this, the quicker we will solve so many of the problems we are facing today, from war to world hunger, inequality, the refugee crises we are facing today, and so much more in between. By understanding this "one-ness," you will solve your internal conflict as well, because everything is intertwined.

You may be asking, why is the Israeli-Palestinian conflict so important? What is so special about a little country in the Middle East that only takes around seven to eight hours to drive through from North to South? Well, here it is in a nutshell. If we solve the Israeli-Palestinian conflict in a just and equitable way, if we stop favoring one people over the other, if we bring peace and justice on equal terms to the table and execute it with honest intentions, we will solve not only this but other issues in the Middle East and globally. Many webs have been weaved and when we solve this conflict and therefore the conflict within each one of us, it will be the catalyst for so many other great things to be resolved. This will include our views on the environment, ending animal cruelty, and making significant changes to humanity. Ask yourself this question: if we can't treat each other with dignity and equality, why do you think we will be able to treat other animals and the environment any better? It's all connected.

Critical Mass

When I first heard you need critical mass to influence real change, my heart sank. It felt like an almost impossible task. The topic of Palestine and Israel is so divisive; you hear people saying things like, "It's too complicated," "It can never be resolved," or "The Palestinians/Israelis will never win." Most people assume there has to be a winner and a loser. Then when you have a look at the political, financial, and military support the Israeli government receives from the Allied world, it feels even more like an impossible task.

But as Nelson Mandela put it so eloquently, "It only seems impossible till it is done." This "conflict" has only been going on for a relatively short time (since 1948). Just because it feels hard to solve does not mean it actually is.

Everything has a beginning and an end. Where once there were dinosaurs, there are now only dragonflies. Over the centuries so many great empires have fallen. There was the rise and fall of the Roman Empire, the decline of the British Empire, and more recently the bringing down of the Berlin Wall, and the end of South African apartheid. At the moment it may feel like nothing will ever change and there is no end to current situations and infrastructures, but over time, everything changes, whether it is a very slow, gradual change, or it comes to what feels like an abrupt end. It's not a question of whether things will change or end, it's a question of *how* we want things to end or change. Do we want it to end in a way whereby we all suffer and lose, or one in which we all gain? Change is inevitable and is the one constant since time began, yet we as humans tend to be surprised by change and often resist it.

So, here is the good news. Shortly after learning about critical mass and the impact it has on real change, I learned critical mass need not be more than 5% of people to start the change process and have an effect. We have to find the other tigers and lions around us. If we want to make a change, focus on finding the 5% of people who have opened their eyes and want to make a change for the better based on equal terms and justice—there is our lowest-hanging fruit—rather than trying to convince people and argue with them. This is how you end the conflict.

This is how South Africa's apartheid was dismantled. Eventually, everyone will follow and open their eyes. This is how we saw the introduction of same-sex marriage in so many countries. This is how the women's rights movement continues to get stronger and stronger. It's how the Black Lives Matter movement was catapulted onto the global stage recently. It's the domino effect at its best.

A Catalyst

It takes just one event to act as the catalyst for change. The catalyst in the "Black Lives Matter" movement was when George Floyd was murdered in May 2020, which was followed by nationwide protests against systemic racism in policing. The moment the late George Floyd pleading with the police was captured on video, where you could visibly see him in distress and crying out, "I can't breathe," was the moment we then felt the impact on social media, which went viral around the world. What followed was huge public outcry, followed by mass protests in countries all over the world.

This one moment built on and strengthened the efforts of the Black Lives Matter movement to promote a broader understanding of systemic racism. We all witnessed each domino tip and knock over the next in sequence. There were months of social action globally, keeping racial justice in our headlines on mainstream media and social media. These mass public demonstrations across the world led to corporate and government commitments to bring about racial equality. We have not seen the end of this yet as the dominoes are still falling one by one.[3]

But let's understand this, the chances of such situations being supported by the powers that be, to begin with, are not high. Many of them have too much at stake right now and too much to lose to stand up for the truth. This is even truer for the Israeli-Palestinian situation. It is the average person in the street in each country who will make a difference and when we collect the critical mass needed, it will place the right pressure on those in positions of power so as to make the necessary change. People have just got to be able to say, *"enough is enough!"*

So, first let's look at the story and what has happened. Let's look at and try to understand why people are behaving the way they are, why they are resorting to such extreme measures, and what is the solution. Knowledge and awareness are power. Once you have awareness, much of the job is complete. There is not a lot more to do. This is for any part of your personal life as well as the great big challenges we face globally and collectively today. The goal here is to assist each individual in their own life by shedding light on one of the most mishandled "conflicts" in modern times and its solution. Surely, when we end the conflict within ourselves, we can end the conflict we see externally.

∾

Chapter 3

THE STORY

What We Believe

When discussing the Israeli-Palestinian issue, the biggest challenge we see today is the inordinate amount of time spent on past events and justifying what has taken place. It can feel like you are watching a long, never-ending tennis match. It's almost as if the world has become desensitized to the whole affair as a result. You can almost feel the eyes rolling, shoulders shrugging, and people putting their hands up in the air as they unconsciously differentiate between the value of one human life when compared to another.

Not Just an Eye for an Eye

The struggle goes on daily, yet you barely hear of the real stories of human tragedy in the news, or if you do, military and government PR teams are rolled out with their excuses and rhetoric. On May 15th 2021, an eleven-story residential building housing sixty people with some media offices and one working elevator was bombed in Gaza by the military giving people less than one hour to evacuate. Children and elderly had to be evacuated, equipment needed to be saved, and a plea for an additional fifteen minutes to evacuate was point-blank rejected by the Isreal Defense Forces (IDF).[1] The Israeli military claimed they have reason to believe the building was harboring Hamas militants, yet there has never been any evidence to prove this point. Four young boys were killed while playing football on the beach in Gaza near a hotel that was housing foreign media representatives, and it is claimed again that Hamas is to blame.[2] Muhammad al-Durrah, a father shielding his son from IDF gunshots while hiding behind a barrel, was executed along with his young son. The IDF initially claimed Palestinians used their children as human shields. Thirteen years after the killing, Benjamin Netanyahu suggested the entire event may have been staged and Mr. al-Durrahwas was not killed, or even injured, even though it was caught on camera and both father and son have been buried.[3] Imagine if this was happening in Ukraine and how the media and governments would respond to Russia today.

When discussing the situation, deflection is merely a tactic used to continue the occupation and ethnic cleansing of Palestinians.

To understand the situation and what is happening today, we need to go back to examine what brought us to where we are today. This will help us understand why we are here and what needs to happen to move forward in a way that improves the quality of life for all people.

While I will stick to basic facts, I am acutely aware of my own stories and biases. There will be times when I may offend people from all sides of the equation. There may be times when people will disagree with me or think I am brushing over a subject. This is a natural part of human life. We must work to overcome our own prejudices and blind spots and listen to understand another's point of view without having to defend ourselves. It is all part of the journey and part of our collective triumph.

If you do a Google search on the chronology of Jewish history and then one on Palestinian history, you would be forgiven to think it's a jumbled mess. You could argue the whole area has a rich history of invasion after invasion, battle after battle, which extended to Europe, and then the colonized world. The history of humans and their constant battles have not been so kind.

If you think we are in a mess today, you just have to look at history since it has all been recorded and you realize there has always been a brutal side to the human race. It's not getting worse today, it's just that we now see events unfold in real time, no matter where it is happening in the world, and we can annihilate ourselves with a single push of a button.

Who Has a Right to Be There?

There is no denying the right for Judaism to exist in the Holy Land, the area known as Palestine before 1948. This is where it was born. Over the centuries, Jews were expelled from the region and have faced many battles in many parts of the world both in ancient times and in modern history. Jews have lived on every continent across the world since their ancestors were expelled by the Romans in 135 AD, and they have been systematically persecuted in many countries and different instances. Wars raged in every continent across the world and those who fell paid a heavy price.[4]

The main difference for Judaism as a religion is Jews today see themselves as a people, and they have sought to reunify and keep their culture and tradition across the globe. This has been their plight and their battle. To explain their history, they will go back through the centuries and are well-versed on all events affecting them.

Modern Zionism was officially established as a political movement by Theodor Herzl, an atheist himself, in 1897. Herzl believed the Jewish population couldn't survive if it didn't have a nation of its own.[5] At that time the Jewish population around the world was approximately 7.7 million, with 90% residing in Europe.[6] This modern Zionism had one single aim—to unify all Jews around the world and for the establishment of a homeland for them.

It's easy to understand the narrative of Jewish people everywhere. Europe, the United Kingdom, and even the United States were not kind to them. They were banned from being included in many parts of society and ostracized by local communities in many instances throughout history.

The Holocaust during Hitler's reign was one of the most grotesque acts of human evil we have seen. Let's be very clear, this is not something that can ever be forgotten, underplayed, or denied. Zionism, though, ensures that the Jewish people remind everyone of the atrocities they have endured throughout history in a different way than how we are taught history at school. Zionism separates the Jewish pain from all others. There are monuments commemorating the events in history in just about every major country. With so many Jewish directors and actors in Hollywood, there are many movies reminding us of all of the events. From the outside looking in, one could say the global Jewish community is one of the most diverse and strongest single groups in the world.

Yet, over the centuries as a community, they experienced ongoing persecution, in many instances being blamed for the actions of those in power, while having very little personal power as individuals. Since its inception, it appears Zionism has had a pervasive influence on global politics, the media, the entertainment industry and its lobby groups. It holds great prominence in the world's banking hierarchies, has a stronghold on the global diamond industry as well as the import and export trade of the most powerful weapons the world over, not to mention secret service operations, both nationally and internationally. The current Zionist government is well-established globally, and it would seem that its primary goal is to fund its military operations, as well as continuing to establish its illegal settlements at any cost, which, ultimately, is at the expense of the Palestinian people, and at the expense of all those opposing their strategic direction.

To do this, it has to keep its people living in fear. It has to separate its people from the rest of the world. And it has to create an "us against the world" scenario. For the Israeli Zionist regime to exist and continue to do what it is doing, it has to keep the fear and the guilt alive in its people.

This tactic is not unique to any single government. It's a tactic that has been used by governments all around the world throughout the ages. There was the Soviet Union's widespread propaganda campaign to scare its citizens into believing that Western values would threaten their way of life. Or the U.S. government's use of the "War on Terror" to justify costly military actions and increased scrutiny of its people's activity.

Fear keeps people obedient. Obedient followers are needed for the survival of regimes. Some governments have played the fear card when it comes to Islam and "terrorism." Once, the fear card was communism, and that remains to be in some areas. In certain countries, that fear card is the West. Right now, the China fear card is being played: the American government and its allies are attempting to scare and unite their community by highlighting potential human rights violations in China such as the suppression of free speech and religious practices, the use of forced labor, and the mass surveillance of its citizens. They further suggest that trade deals with China put U.S. jobs and interests at risk. Thus, the fear tactics continue to spin, like a revolving door.

Many Jews will attest that Zionism emerged from origins of pure and well-intentioned beliefs, and its single aim was to protect the core values of its people who had been persecuted for so long. We can all understand this. You just have to do a quick Google search and you will find an extensive list of every event in which Jewish people were persecuted en masse. The fear can be easily substantiated, but the need to have a haven for the Jews alone only took effect once modern Zionism had been well-established. Prior to that time, there was no real incentive to have a country for the Jewish people alone.

In 1799, during the siege on Acre, Napoleon Bonaparte proclaimed that the Jews were the "rightful heirs of Palestine" to gain the support of the Jews residing there. It is believed that most Jews in Palestine, especially in Jerusalem, were fearful of the French and assisted the Turks instead, regardless of his promises.[7] Even Jews from different parts of the world did not necessarily think they belonged to one homeland. German Jews considered themselves German, American Jews saw themselves as American, and Palestinian Jews as Palestinian. Thus, they did not necessarily support Napoleon's offer for a Jewish state in Palestine. It was not until modern Zionism and the fear it instilled in its followers that we saw this need for a homeland for all Jewish people, separate from everyone else.

With the advent of modern Zionism, it was clear that the founders from the outset did not see non-Jewish Palestinians as having any rightful claims to live side by side with the Palestinian Jews. Jews, Christians, and Muslims had coexisted on the land of Palestine together for centuries. To coexist meant that all people who resided in Palestine had to have fought the same battles at some stage, had to have been invaded by the same empires, and must have suffered the same or equally atrocious losses. The area had been invaded, raped, and pillaged so often throughout history that no individual group of people can ever claim a monopoly on the suffering that has prevailed. This is not an attempt to minimize any one people's pain. It is to illustrate that all nations throughout history have suffered many devastating and sustained losses.

Throughout the centuries, Palestine and the whole region have been invaded and oppressed by various empires and powers seeking to gain control and expand their own dominion. From the Assyrians to the Babylonians, the Persians to the Ottomans, and subsequently, the European colonists, which included the British occupation, the people of the Middle East have endured endless hardship and battles as their land was carved up, divided and weakened by the various interlopers.

The list of invaders in Palestine is a long one and the point of mentioning it is to help you understand that all people, in all the lands that were conquered, were persecuted and felt a great deal of pain. There was migration, there was pillaging, and civilians were terrorized at the hands of their conquerors or colonizers. There were also constant changes to political expectations and allegiance. During

Ottoman rule, as an example, my grandfather would have been forced to fight in Gallipoli against the Allies simply due to the occupation of Palestine by the Ottomans until the end of the First World War. There is a story of one of my grandfathers (he was my father's uncle, but as kids, we knew him as "Sido," which means Granddad), trying to flee the Ottoman military service only to be caught and brought back to fight against his will.

Even after the UN declared genocide a war crime in 1951, over the following 50 years, millions have been killed by genocide worldwide. During the twentieth century alone, it is estimated that over 20 million people have died by genocide.[8] Pain is shared by all.

What was different about the Zionist movement in Europe is while it claimed to work towards protecting its people, *it denied the rights of any other people in Palestine.* The now-infamous Balfour Declaration, a public pledge signed by the British on November 2, 1917, supported the establishment in Palestine of a national home for the Jewish people. Zionism had already adopted the slogan that Palestine was a land without a people, and the Jews were a people without a land.

In the words of Palestinian scholar, Edward Said, this was a declaration "made by a European power...about a non-European territory...in a flat disregard of both the presence and wishes of the native majority resident in that territory."[9] Its severe ramifications are still felt today.

A Homeland

Regardless of whether or not you agree that the Jewish people needed a homeland, whether or not European and American Jews belonged in Palestine, or whether they had the right to claim land after more than 2000 years, *they* believed it, which is something we do need to acknowledge. Nonetheless, this was no longer about the survival of one group of people only. This was about the colonization of one land by a group of people at the expense of another. They declared the buzzing and thriving country of Palestine, "a land without a people." This statement is very much an unreality given that the inhabitants had been there for thousands of years. This fictitious claim was made by early Zionist settlers in the late nineteenth and early twentieth centuries. However, the Palestinian people had already formed their own national identity and culture; their major cities were vibrant commercial hubs for the Middle East and Europe. They were well-known for their scholars, and their music; roads, trade, and a legal system were already firmly established and well-documented. Given that this actual reality was ignored and completely dismissed clearly shows the intention and aggression about to be laid upon the Palestinian population in the twentieth century. The erroneous claim of "a land without a people" was used to justify the establishment of a Jewish state in Palestine and led to the displacement and dispossession of the Palestinian people.

Before the Balfour Declaration, which was a result of the British wanting to secure European Jewish support during World War I[10] , the Palestinian Jewish population was between eight and ten percent of the total population.[11] They were a part of the holistic cultural structure and lived in relative harmony as part of the ecosystem with the remaining Palestinian Muslims, Christians, Druze, Bedouins, and others who made up ninety to ninety-two percent of the total population.

This Declaration is now a century old, but its effects continue to have widespread repercussions today. Britain's colonial legacy may seem like it's a thing of the past and ancient history, but it has, and remains to have, catastrophic effects on Palestinians, and in surrounding countries of the Middle East as well as in the West.

Chapter 4

THE TRUTH

What We All Have in Common

"Computers are useless: they can only give you answers."

— *Pablo Picasso*

F or us to decipher what the ultimate truth is, in any situation, we must first ask certain questions of ourselves. It is the quality of our questions that determines the quality of our lives, leadership, and future.

Seeking Solutions / Asking Questions to Eradicate Personal Bias

If you want to focus on solutions for yourself and for our world, it is the questions that you ask yourself that will help you find the way, not the answers you think you already know. Often when I find myself in a situation where I don't know what to do, rather than looking for an answer that I do not have, I ask questions of myself. These questions include:

- What am I not seeing?
- How can I look at this situation differently?
- How can I see it from the other person's point of view?
- What do I want to believe?
- Who can help me to see things differently?
- What if I am wrong?

This list is not an all-inclusive one, but it is a good place to start. There are times when such questions can be difficult and uncomfortable to put out there, so just allow yourself to sit with them, feel them, and don't feel like you have to come up with an answer straight away. Expect these ponderings will challenge your paradigms but given that all paradigms are based on your inner belief system, there will always be something new that you have, as yet, not considered. Just be open to entertaining new ideas. Regardless, you can accept or reject ideas at any time. So why not be open to new information? Why be closed-minded when we know that there are so many different angles from which to view and perceive any one situation?

According to Dr. Joseph Dispenza, in the 2006 documentary film *What the Bleep...Down the Rabbit Hole,* "The brain processes 400 billion bits of information a second, but we are only aware of 2,000 of those." Which 2,000 bits will depend on a few factors such as our environment, what we have been brought up to believe, our own experiences, and our DNA, to name a few. Our minds at a subconscious level will quickly look for and choose those 2,000 bits of information based on what we have known from the past, and what feels familiar. In essence, if we allow our subconscious mind to do all the heavy lifting, we will never question anything new and we will keep on interpreting any given situation based on what we already know.

It's a bit like the experiment on the Netflix show *Magic for Humans,* where an actor approaches a person on the street and asks for directions. While the person was consulting a map, they switched out the actor for a completely different actor, wearing the same outfit. Almost nobody noticed the difference after the swap. Why is that?

Simply put, we are so locked into that limited number of bits of information that we become aware of, based on what we already know, everything else goes unnoticed.

Can you see the dilemma we have here? As human beings, if we keep searching for past experiences, all we will do is create our future from the familiar past. This is why we keep repeating the same mistakes.

The People of the Book

If you try to make sense of this estimated number of 2,000 bits of information, it is staggering as to how much we are not aware of at any given time. If we are only aware of a microscopic fraction of the information to which we are exposed, and yet we desire to evolve and grow, then we have to question what is being presented to us. As human beings, we have so much more to learn and to expand upon, yet it seems we are limiting ourselves considerably. This applies to every single person no matter what side of the "fence" we think we are sitting on. Therefore, here are some questions to start the process and where, with regard to Palestine and her people, it all supposedly began.

- Do we believe thousands of years ago God chose one group of people over all the other groups of people?
- Do we believe God promised one group of people the land exclusively?
- Did God act as the landlord at this time?
- If God did so, which land was he referring to?
- While God was giving these instructions so specifically, why did he not give equally specific instructions as to what to do with all the other people at the time, and thereafter, on this same land?
- If he did, why did we choose not to listen to that part?

What God Wants

Reading *What God Wants* (2005) by Neale Donald Walsch, cemented it all for me. In his book, Neale asks the question on numerous occasions, "What does God want?"[1] There are over 400 religions in this world. All of them agree on one fundamental point. God exists. What we don't seem to agree on is which religion is the right religion. Which one should you follow to lead you to the gates of heaven? This, of course, is said with tongue firmly in cheek.

So, the next question is, do we think that out of the 400-plus religions, there is only one faith that God will accept to enter through the gates of heaven? Are we actually going to subscribe to that theory? There was a time, not too long ago when a person would be persecuted as a Christian for asking these questions. To this day, you can be ostracized by many organized religious groups for questioning the "written" word of God. Yet where has it gotten us so far?

With regard to the written word, Jews, Christians, and Muslims (in that order), are said to all be "the people of the book," and all believe that there is only one God. They all believe in the same God. As a Palestinian, you grow up knowing that all three religions believe in the one God only. The prayers are sung each day in synagogues, churches, and mosques as they have been for centuries.

"Hear, Israel: the LORD is our **God**, the LORD is **one**"
– Beginning of the Shema reading recited twice daily in Jewish prayer.

"Yet for us, there is **one God**, the Father, from whom are all things and for whom we exist, and one Lord, Jesus Christ, through whom are all things and through whom we exist."
– 1 Corinthians 8:6 English Standard Version (ESV) of the Bible

God is the **Greatest.** There is **no God** but **God Himself**
– According to Islam.

It always fascinates me when I see Christians from the West react to Muslim prayers and chants. The media takes footage of crowds chanting "Allahu Akbar," and in the West, many people fear it and associate it with terrorism. Yet the word "Allah" is the Arabic word for God. No matter what your religion is, if you speak Arabic, you will always refer to God as Allah. It is not a Muslim word. It is an Arabic word. In Hebrew, the word for God is Elohim. So, if I am speaking in English, I will refer to the Almighty as God, or Our Lord. If I am speaking in Arabic, it will be Allah or Rabuna (Our Lord), and in Hebrew Elohim or Adonai (My Lord). In short, when we take a chronological look at the appearance of religions in the geographical area of the Holy Land from the River Jordan to the Mediterranean Sea, Judaism was first, then Christianity, followed by Islam. One could say there was an attempt to evolve. Modern-day Palestinian Christians may have converted from Judaism to Christianity given that Jesus was from Palestine, and Jewish. And Palestinian Muslims may have converted (reverted, according to Islam) from Christianity. Why they converted could be for several reasons; however, the point is our origins and roots in the land are of equal relevance to all three religions.

No one religion is right or wrong. They share much in common. Jews, Christians, and Muslims have lived together in relative harmony on one land for centuries. It's in our DNA to live together. So where did it all go wrong?

In the awareness of contrast, fear, and injustice, we can find love and peace. There is no greater contrast, and pain, than the modern-day Palestinian plight. This is not a 2,000-year-old conflict. It is a modern-day struggle born from manipulation, fear, and greed.

It is by rejecting the current narrative that we can forge a life full of love, abundance, and acceptance. By understanding and being aware of what is happening, the path to great leadership, freedom, peace, prosperity and belonging is possible and may only be around the corner for us all. It is all Palestinians have wanted since 1948.

Innately, that is all each of us wants. We all want to be free to do the things that bring us joy. We want to be with the people who raise us up (providing a sense of belonging) and to share that joy with them. Furthermore, we want to have enough to be able to enjoy it all (prosperity).

In some ways, every single one of us from all over the world is "Palestinian" looking for truth, belonging, freedom, and prosperity.

∾

Chapter 5

THE REALITY

From the Oppressed to the Oppressor

I magine yourself as a parent with ten young children, and all of a sudden, you are warned to leave your home and land—to take only your absolutely necessary belongings and flee. You don't have much time to decide whether you will try to escape across the border or run and hide amid the olive plantations, seeking refuge and protection. You've just heard there have been mass shootings and deaths at a nearby village and in your heart, you know you must leave everything behind to save your family.

What would you do? How would you react if you and your loved ones suddenly realized your lives were in danger, that your deeds, legal documents/titles, land, furniture, and even clothes had to be left behind to save your lives? How would you feel if you refused to leave your home, only to have all the men rounded up, forced to face a wall, and shot in the back of the head? They would then be thrown into an unmarked hole in the ground and buried with others, just to send a message out to the remaining villages and cities of what was about to happen to them should they resist.

Does this only happen in movies? Is this story for real? Can the oppressed all of a sudden become the oppressor? Unfortunately, it is a true story. This has been the Palestinian story since 1948, the start of the Nakba (the catastrophe). This was my grandparents' story with their ten children who chose to hide in the olive groves and then seek shelter rather than cross the border, yet still they lost their home and belongings. My mother was six years old. My father was eleven years old, and his family also chose to flee Haifa to a nearby village for protection, rather than try and cross the borders. They, too, lost everything in Haifa. This is the pain etched into every Palestinian's heart, but it was only the beginning of the catastrophe, the horror of which still endures today. Yet it is ignored and swept under the carpet by Western governments, mainly because they continue to play an explicit part in this drama. As Malcolm X put it so clearly, "If you're not careful, the newspapers will have you hating the people who are being oppressed and loving the people who are doing the oppressing." This is exactly what is happening to the Palestinian people today.

Undeniable Horror

World War II had a horrific impact on Jews in Europe. Hitler had ordered his troops to systematically round up the Jewish people in Germany, and areas he had successfully taken over, and subsequently have them sent to concentration camps. The way it was carried out over the years was slow and strategic. The goal was to wipe out the Jewish people. At first, Jews were ordered to wear yellow stars to identify themselves. The fear-mongering campaigns enabled Hitler to carry out his long-term plans against the Jewish population. Many Jews in Germany and neighboring regions saw the signs early on and fled to Palestine, England, America, and other countries.

It is estimated that over 6 million Jews perished in the concentration camps.[1] Before Hitler's takeover of power in 1933, Europe had a vibrant, well-established, and very diverse Jewish culture. By the end of his reign in 1945, it is further estimated in Europe, two out of every three Jews had been killed.

The Nazi regime was brutal by nature, and what they subjected their victims to was horrendous and unimaginable. World War II was the most destructive war in history with an estimated 40 to 50 million people being killed. This figure has been noted as high as 60 million or more by some. Civilian casualties accounted for a huge percentage of this figure.[2] When people say "never again," we need to make sure it is never again for everyone; otherwise, the cycle of violence will perpetuate. What happened after World War II was just a continuation of the devastation. Palestine, like its neighboring countries, was also hard-hit by the war and its aftereffects.

Britain had occupied Palestine since the Arab uprising against the Ottomans and the end of World War I. The British had promised Palestinians eventual independence as a result of their loyalty to Britain against the Ottomans. The Belfour declaration to gain Jewish support, in particular for American Jews, further complicated the situation. Britain lost control of the many events taking place in Palestine between the local inhabitants and the increasing number of European Jewish refugees who were welcomed by Palestinians initially.

Zionism

In the meantime, the Zionist Movement was preparing to take over the land of Palestine, and different plans on what to do with the majority of the non-Jewish population living there were set up. These plans are well-documented today and we can see the main proposal was to expel the non-Jewish Palestinian population to Jordan and other Arab countries.

By this stage, the Jewish Resistance Movement had formed. Several attacks and bombings against the British administration in Palestine were carried out, including the bombing of the King David

Hotel in Jerusalem (1946). This event was seen as "an important milestone in the evolution and internationalization of terrorism."[3]

In 1948, the UN mediator, Count Bernadotte, was assassinated in Jerusalem. The British Mandate was becoming unpopular in Britain, and as a result, the United States Congress delayed granting the British the required financial support for reconstruction. The British government had reneged on its promise before its own election in 1945 to allow mass Jewish migration. As a result, anti-British Jewish militant efforts increased, resulting in an influx of over 100,000 British troops into Palestine. With the influx of European Jewish migrants into the country, the continued upheaval, and the lack of support, the British decided to withdraw from Palestine. They set the date of August 1948 to end the Mandate.

It was then that the British called upon the UN asking what should be done regarding the situation in Palestine. In brief, eleven countries voted to have the country divided into two separate states with Jerusalem coming under international law. Three countries voted to have one state for all, while Australia abstained from the vote. Part of this partition plan was to grant full civil rights to all people within their borders, regardless of race, religion, or gender.

The Official End of Palestine

Unsurprisingly, Palestinians at the time did not support this plan and saw it as a real threat to their existence, leading to the Arab-Israeli war. At midnight on May 15, 1948, the State of Israel was created. The Palestinian government formally ended, the Palestine police force was immediately disbanded, and non-Jewish Palestinians lost all protection. The 1948 Palestinian exodus/Nakba (Catastrophe) was born. Palestinians have been fighting for their rights ever since with the international community turning a blind eye to the humanitarian crises created.

This situation continues to worsen as the current Israeli government gains more power and executes its original plans, despite it being in contravention of international law. From the Jordan River to the Mediterranean Sea was always the goal of the Modern Zionist movement, at any cost and with no regard for the non-Jewish Indigenous population of the land.

∼

Chapter 6

THE CATASTROPHE (NAKBA)

Not Your Home Anymore

"A lie gets halfway around the world
before the truth puts on its boots."
—*Winston Churchill*

(NAKBA) refers to the The Forced Expulsion

You know you have a home, a bed to come home to. But imagine that tonight you are told to take what you can carry and leave. What would you take? Where would you go? Maybe you will get to come back, but maybe not. Hold that thought for a moment. Most of us can't even conceive of that. We know we have a right to be in our homes, we built them, paid for them, earned our possessions, treasure the lives we live. It is unquestionable.

Many people, including many of my Jewish friends at one point, believed a myth about the creation of Israel, suggesting that Palestinians willingly packed their bags and abandoned their homes, generously making way for the Jews to settle in a civilized manner. But, for myself and all Palestinians, this narrative is deeply emotional because the truth is that they were forcefully uprooted. It's hard for me to understand how people can still deny the events. This distortion of history, especially the events of 1948, is a painful denial as the Palestinian experience is often overlooked or intentionally erased. As one very close Jewish friend explained to me, this is a survival mechanism and even she herself feels ashamed of how she did not see this early on in her young adult life as the New State of Israel was established.

When my grandparents hid under the olive trees, before seeking refuge in a nearby village with other family members, my grandmother Saada took her large house key with her as one of the few belongings they gathered before fleeing, thinking she would be returning to her home within a couple of weeks. When they returned a year later, along with their ten children, they quickly realized everything was gone and they were forced to move into a small place under the old Protestant church in Haifa's Wadi Il Nisnas. My grandmother passed away, when I was six months old, of a broken heart. She was buried with the key to her home that she was never allowed to return to. She walked past it on many occasions over the years, only to see a foreign family living there who had taken the house and everything in it. This is why Palestinians say Israel seized Palestine "fully furnished." Everything was taken and looted. From clothes to spoons, and even the meals that were being cooked on the stove and left as people fled their homes in fear for their lives. The whole infrastructure was taken as it stood, from airports to schools, shops to lands with crops, and everything in between.

Never Again—Not to Us

"If I don't steal it, someone else will."

What actually took place was that the Zionist military forcibly expelled at least 750,000 Palestinians from their homes and lands; by 1967, they captured 78% of what was then called Palestine. The remaining 22% was divided into what we now know as the military-occupied West Bank and the Gaza Strip. Gaza has since been dubbed by former British Prime Minister David Cameron, Palestinians, and many humanitarians, as the largest open-air prison and concentration camp in the world.[1]

For Palestinians, the Nakba is not an event that has happened in the past. The Nakba is a process that continues to displace them daily, and has never stopped. The ethnic cleansing of non-Jewish Palestinians, which began with the mass eviction in the 1940s, created a refugee crisis that continues to affect millions of Palestinians today. The unresolved political situation, the Israeli occupation of Palestinian territories, and the lack of a viable solution for Palestinian refugees contribute to the ongoing nature of the Nakba. The annual Nakba Day protests are a reminder that the Palestinian people's struggle for justice and the right to return to their homeland remains unfulfilled. To this day, Palestinians are forcibly removed from their homes and not allowed to return, so as to accommodate Jewish settlers from abroad on illegally occupied land.[2]

In a recent Sheikh Eljarra case, a video went viral featuring a New York-born Jewish settler named Yaakov (originally Jason) Fauci. He was confronted by a Palestinian woman from the Al-Kurd family in East Jerusalem, as he occupied their property. In the video, Fauci defended his right to stay and dismissed the woman's claims. When asked about his occupation, he bluntly stated, "If I don't steal it, someone else will." This incident sparked international outrage as it highlighted the Palestinian plight in such a simple way.

When you hear someone say the situation is complicated, this is where we must say: "*Stop*. It is not complicated at all."

In seeking a solution to the Jewish dilemma and dream, the Palestinian predicament and catastrophe were created. Between 1947 and 1949, over 530 villages were destroyed, and major Palestinian cities were attacked. It is estimated over 15,000 Palestinians were killed in a series of attacks and dozens of massacres, including the Deir Yassin massacre where 110 men, women, and children were murdered by the Zionist militia.[3]

The right to return has a strong foundation in international law. Article 13(2) of the Universal Declaration of Human Rights (UDHR) states, "Everyone has the right to leave any country, including his own, and to return to his country."[4] Israel does not permit displaced Palestinians to return to their legally owned homes and lands. The plight of the Palestinian refugees is one of the longest and harshest in the world.

Gaza Under Siege

The Gaza Strip has been under both land and sea blockades since 2007. Over 2.3 million people live in a 365-square-kilometer space and is highly controlled by the Israeli military. Since 2008 and at the time of this writing, Israel has waged four wars on Gaza, killing thousands of people. It claims the threat of Hamas to the existence of Israel, one of the strongest military powers in our current world, is too great.

Medical aid, raw materials, concrete, water, electricity, and food are all controlled by the Israeli military. In 2006 and after the election of Hamas, it was reported that a senior Israeli official described Israel's planned response as "to put the Palestinians on a diet, but not to cause them to die of hunger."

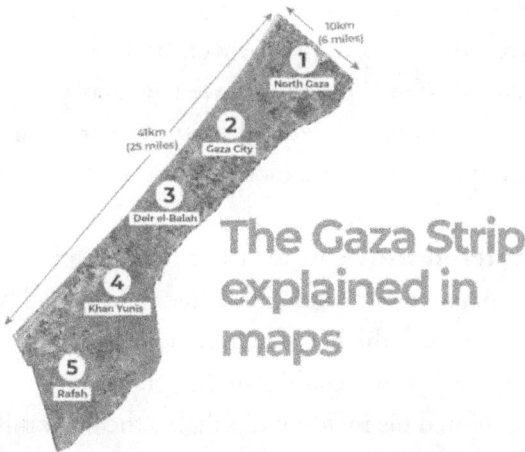

This was, of course, denied until Israel was forced to disclose a government research document drafted in 2008 where health officials provided calculations of the minimum number of calories needed by Gaza's then 1.5 million population to avoid malnutrition.

As of 2023 there are over 2.3 million people living in Gaza. Those figures were translated into truckloads of food that the Israeli military was supposed to allow to enter Gaza each day. Gisha, an Israeli not-for-profit organization, founded in 2005, was the organization that fought for the document's publication. They wanted to show not only had the number of calories been calculated to avoid malnutrition, but also that there was a further restriction placed on nearly half of those trucks entering Gaza, which had a severe impact on the population on many fronts, including their ability to grow crops inside Gaza.[5]

Under Military Occupation and the Violations of International Humanitarian Law

Of those living under military occupation in the West Bank, over 3.2 million Palestinians have had every single part of their lives impacted by the services they can access, travel, and even where they are allowed to live or who they are allowed to marry. The Al–Kurd's family experience is not isolated. The list of restrictions grows every day. Some examples of these include, but are not limited to:

- **Restricted movement**: In 2015, a pregnant Palestinian woman named Ghadeer Abu Jamal was unable to reach the hospital in time due to delays at an Israeli checkpoint, resulting in her giving birth at the checkpoint. This incident highlights the daily difficulties Palestinians face when trying to access healthcare and other essential services.
- **Isolation of communities:** The village of Qusra in the West Bank is surrounded by several illegal Israeli settlements and outposts. These settlements have led to land confiscations, restricted movement, and limited access to resources for the village residents, isolating them completely from other Palestinian communities.

- **Loss of land and resources**: In 2020, Israel approved the construction of 7,000 new settlement homes in the West Bank, further expanding its presence on Palestinian land. These expansions directly impact Palestinian farmers who lost or have yet to lose their agricultural lands and livelihoods.
- **Discriminatory policies:** In 2018, a report found that Israeli settlers in the West Bank consumed over three times more water per capita than their Palestinian neighbors. This disparity significantly impacts Palestinians' ability to maintain proper sanitation, agriculture, and overall quality of life.
- **Economic challenges:** In 2019, the World Bank reported the Palestinian economy in the West Bank faced a 15% unemployment rate and 24% poverty rate. The occupation's restrictions on movement, trade, and resources contribute to these economic challenges. The unemployment rate in Gaza is significantly higher than that.
- **Human rights violations:** In January 2021, an Israeli settler shot and killed a Palestinian man while he was working on his land near the village of Ras Karkar in the West Bank. This is just one example of the violence and human rights abuses Palestinians face under the occupation.

These examples[6] go on and on with seemingly no end to the Israeli government's abuse of Palestinians living under the occupation. These have been documented by several organizations including Human Rights Watch and B'Tselem. The abuses include:

- Continued land and property theft
- Illegal demolition of homes (8,413 between 2009 and 2022)

- Forcible transfers and displacement
- Severe movement restrictions aided by a multitude of military checkpoints, walls, and enclosures
- Illegal killings
- Detainment of children by the police and military courts with no representation
- Torture
- Administrative detention
- The continued denial of citizenship for Palestinians.[7]

These are all violations of international humanitarian law (IHL) and international human rights law.[8]

What is also a violation of international law is the continued growth of illegal settlements on Palestinian land, as briefly mentioned previously. There are estimated to be 750,000 Israeli settlers living in 250 illegal settlements in the occupied territories, with little to no protection from regular settler attacks. The population of settlers is growing faster than the population of Jews in Israel due to the government support, aid, and subsidies handed out to the settlers.

A "Democratic" Israel: How We Got This Way

After the expulsion of 750,000 Palestinians in the 1948 to 1949 war, approximately 150,000 remained in the border areas of the newly founded state of Israel. Those remaining Palestinians lived under an oppressive military rule that restricted their movement, freedom of speech, and ability to work from 1949 to 1966. In 1967, they were granted Israeli citizenship. Israel claims to be the only democracy in the Middle East. Today the number of Palestinians living in what is termed as "Israel Proper" is just over 2 million. They are classified as "Arab Israelis" and refused the right to identify themselves as Palestinian. For a long time, even calling yourself Palestinian could mean a jail term. They represent approximately 20% of the total population in "democratic" Israel and are allowed to vote.

To maintain the Jewish majority, Israel has created several laws to control the growth of these Palestinians with voting rights. There are over sixty-five laws that discriminate against the Palestinian citizens of Israel directly or indirectly, according to Adalah, the Legal Centre for Arab Minority Rights in Israel. They are based solely on their ethnicity and impact all areas of their lives from housing, employment, education, health care, and who they can marry.[9] The Human Rights Watch issued a report in May 2020, titled *Israel: Discriminatory Land Policies Hem In Palestinians; Palestinian Towns Squeezed While Jewish Towns Grow*. It stated:

"Decades of land confiscations and discriminatory planning policies have confined many Palestinian citizens to densely populated towns and villages that have little room to expand. Meanwhile, the Israeli government nurtures the growth and expansion of neighboring predominantly Jewish communities, many built on the ruins of Palestinian villages destroyed in 1948."[10]

It is believed the original plan, known as Plan Dalet (on March 10, 1948, in Tel Aviv), formed by Zionist political and military leaders, including David Ben-Gurion, was to rid the newly formed state of all non-Jewish Indigenous inhabitants systematically: village by village, city by city. In 1967 Ben Gurion, the prime minister at the time, reluctantly offered the remaining 150,000 Palestinians citizenship mainly due to foreign pressure.

Yet, even as early as 1919, U.S. legal scholar Morris Cohen expressed some skepticism concerning the wisdom of Jewish ethnonationalism in *The New Republic*:

"How could a Jewish Palestine allow complete religious freedom, freedom of inter-marriage and free non-Jewish immigration, without soon losing its very reason for existence? A national Jewish Palestine must necessarily mean a state founded on a particular race, a tribal religion, and a mystic belief in a particular soil, whereas liberal America stands for the separation of church and state, the free mixing of races, and that men can change their habitation and language and still advance the process of civilization. Zionists are quite willing to

ignore the rights of the vast majority of the non-Jewish population of Palestine. Whether tribalism triumphs or not, it is nonetheless evil, and thinking men should reject it as such."[11]

~

Part Two

The Heart

Chapter 7

THE SYMPTOM

You Can't Cure a Symptom

*"Never again means never again **for everyone**."*

E verything you've read thus far is just the tip of the iceberg. I won't go any farther down a rabbit hole here, as there is ample documentation to allow people to read up on their own, and to draw their own conclusions.

I am purposely not going into greater convoluted detail that will take us away from the basic root cause of the present predicament, and as mentioned previously, I am not a politician, an academic, nor an historian. I am a human being who happens to have been born a Palestinian, a Christian from the Galilee region, with an Israeli citizenship who grew up around the Palestinian Communist Party and sang in a choir in the churches of the Holy Land. I also lived in England for three years as a child and moved back to Haifa before immigrating to Australia at about fourteen years of age with my immediate family.

Politics did play heavily around me as a child, and it was a case of the have and have-nots, the oppressor and oppressed. All disguised and masked, nothing ever appeared as it was. Everyone had an opinion; everyone believed their view was right and it was always fiercely black and white. People spoke in absolutes and there was never a middle ground. Even with what we are experiencing today globally, speaking in "absolutes" has become prevalent. Is it any wonder we are experiencing even more division and anger worldwide?

The real global pandemic is not a virus, but rather fear and stress. Fear is consuming us, and we are all witness to the resulting division —division and separation in relationships, in society, in business, and, sadly, in leadership. This will never be the answer to freedom, growth, or prosperity.

There were many Jewish people back in the old country who became our close family friends. They had survived Hitler's Holocaust and had rebuilt their lives to become successful influential public figures in the State. They are now helping Palestinians who have been wrongly treated by the system. They could see that somehow the once-oppressed had become the oppressor. One of those family friends was a gentleman by the name of Dr. Bergmann. He used to visit us regularly and played an active role in my mum's work with the visually impaired as well as helping the family when my eldest uncle was imprisoned by the Israeli government and was on trial. He would often come to visit us at home, and I remember the times I spent with him as a youngster, asking him questions. On one of those visits, he showed me the tattoo on his arm from the concentration camps in Germany. As he showed it to me, he said to me, "Reem, this should never again happen to anyone." To this day and over forty-five years later, this one thought goes through my head on repeat, "Never again means never again for everyone."

You must wonder why some people were so openly helpful while many others saw Palestinians as a threat. How could they not see that non-Jewish Palestinians belonged to the same land they were now claiming as their own? Why would they treat non-Jewish Palestinians with such contempt and with no equality? How could people be so cruel to others after what they had just been through?

These close Jewish family friends recognized that the oppressed had become the oppressor purely out of fear and lack of awareness. Those who have contempt for Palestinians and don't see them as equals are blinded by fear. Some people may think the simplicity of the last point is too easy a way out, but it is that simple.

When asked how our friends personally managed to see Palestinians in a different light themselves, the answer was even simpler. By asking themselves questions and opening their hearts, it led them to greater clarity. When you open your heart and ask it the right questions, you can only see, hear, and feel the truth. Everyone has a story and many people from all walks of life have overcome adversity beyond what the mind could fathom. Yet with an open heart and the right questions, you can achieve everything you want to achieve, and most importantly, it does not have to be at the expense of any other human being.

What We Need From Leadership

"We need leaders not in love with money but in love with justice. not in love with publicity but in love with humanity."

— *Dr. Martin Luther King Jr.*

Great leadership needs conscious awareness to keep asking all the right questions with an open heart and mind. The best form of leadership comes from a place of unconditional love, caring, and kindness for each other. Anything else will only bring short-term "wins" with a lot of heartache and pain, for you and those around you.

Here in Australia, I have lived in four different states and have been exposed to many new cultures. I now know what it is like to feel free with opportunities available to me based on my own abilities and desires, regardless of ethnicity or religious beliefs. I have been fortunate enough to be able to question everything I have been taught without retribution, make mistakes as part of my growth, and befriend people from all walks of life with no restrictions.

I can sit with Jews and discuss topics openly as equals, express my feelings and fears, discover how each person feels and understand their fears. It's not always easy to discuss some topics that are raw and run deep in our fear psyche. However, if you work on keeping your heart open, allowing yourself to feel and understand the pain, you will begin to open your eyes to not just your personal plight, but also to the plight of others.

We must reflect to understand, not to find blame and justify our actions. Our minds will always go searching for evidence which supports our beliefs and our cause. But every cause has an effect. What we are seeing in today's world are just symptoms of the real problem, not the problem itself. We keep working on fixing the symptoms based on our beliefs; however, these beliefs come from the data that we choose to see from our history, and we keep trying to cure the symptoms in the same way we have always done; this results in creating even more symptoms.

~

Chapter 8

THE ROOT CAUSE

Where Fear Comes From

The biggest problem in today's world is separation. Most powers don't know this. If they did, why would we be experiencing the turmoil we have today?

We are such an immature species; we keep repeating the same tactics, the same stories, and then using the same supposed solutions and hoping for a different result. The problems that can be attributed to alienation and separation are increasing every day. Every group you can imagine is being alienated in one form or another:

- Rich from poor
- Religion from religion
- State from state
- Country from country
- One ethnicity from another
- One political view from the other
- One team from another in an organizational structure
- Colleagues from other colleagues
- Friends from other friends
- Family members from other family members

Those in power don't understand to what extent the impact that separation is having on our world and our existence. Ironically, this is because they have separated themselves from everyone and everything else, allowing power and ego to get in the way.

Separation is an Illusion

We believe we are separate from each other, and it started back in our caveman days. We realized there were certain things we have no control over, like thunder and lightning, the sun and the moon, flooding, and drought, and other carnivores preying on us for food, and thus tribalism was born. As mammals, we do have a primitive part of our brain that tells us we need to belong to a particular herd to protect and feed ourselves and our loved ones. We do all that we can to remain with the herd by accepting the rules and practices set, without questioning them. If we don't play by the rules and regulations of our tribe, then we fear the loss of protection and possibility of being ostracized—which would make us sitting ducks for our predators. This is entrenched in our psyche at a subconscious level. Due to us believing we are a separate entity from everything around us, we have an incredible need to find and belong to a group; so, for protection, we do anything we can to be favored by those around us.

Eventually, as a result of not understanding those elements beyond our control, religion was born, and it has evolved over the centuries as human consciousness has expanded. But once we separated ourselves, we started to believe there must be a higher power that is external to ourselves. Many religions believe that God is somewhere else, separate from us. Some believe God is in the heavens looking down on us, while we are all down here on Earth. We even made God a male, exhibiting emotions of anger, and we feared the wrath of God. We were then taught that it was necessary to find various ways to ensure that we please God to keep him happy, and to stay on his good side, as it were.

If we look at Judaism, Christianity, and Islam as an example, all three believe in the one God who is looking down on us, protecting us —but also judging us. Are we being good or are we being bad? Are we serving him well, or are we going against his word? Are we doing what God wants? Even though all three religions believe that we came from God, it is also believed that our role is to win back God's favor to be rewarded, not in this life, but in the afterlife in heaven. We created God in our image, not the other way around, and made God behave as humans behave in times of stress and anger, and with an "ego." Therefore, if God can punish us, we think, then surely, we can punish others? Can you imagine what would have happened if we had created an all-loving, peaceful, non-judgemental, and forgiving God? How would we then be able to justify our actions? But if God could be vengeful, then we give ourselves permission to also be the same.

Our separation theology produced a separation cosmology. It told us that we are separate from the universe and all that is in it. Even today, most of us go about our business forgetting that we live on a planet spinning through an immense outer space, which it has done for billions of years. We forget that everything here on Earth—from the most minuscule particle, to the mechanics of the entire universe— runs to absolute precision. Our solar system was not thrown together by chance. The precision with which the solar system, a part of the universe, is designed, is far greater than anything created by humans. Other stars in the solar system have different energy outputs than the Earth's star—the sun. Our sun varies in its energy output by less than one-tenth of one per cent. Life would be impossible if we were orbiting other stars. Even our distance from the sun is precise so as to ensure life on Earth as we know it.

To take it one step further, there are many moons in the solar system and some planets have multiple moons that come in different shapes. The Earth's moon is distinctive in that it is spherical and circles us at a relatively gentle twenty-seven-day orbit. It is the only object other than the sun that influences processes on Earth. The moon moderates the planet's wobble on its axis, which leads to a relatively stable climate. The moon also causes tides that create a rhythm that has helped guide humans for thousands of years.

Separation cosmology creates separation psychology in human beings. Separation psychology is where we believe that we are all separate from each other and everything around us. This is where we start to focus on our bodies as though that is all we are, even though— like the universe—99.99% of our body is made of space.

Separation psychology creates separation sociology. Can you see what we are doing to ourselves? We separate ourselves right from the beginning only to try to find ourselves again through groups. We create societies with entities of their own, separate from other societies. Each society then develops its own set of beliefs and modes of behavior, which is followed by the collective within the same group.

What Unites Us

We need to ask ourselves, what are we doing here? Different religions believe theirs is the one to follow and all other paths will not lead us to eternal salvation. Conservatives in the U.S. and other countries are fiercely dictating who is right and who is wrong. Countries are looking for allies and seem to be preparing their constituents for battle. False news is rampant and arguments over many social issues are at an all-time high. We are fighting each other at a micro and macro level in all parts of our lives.

This separation of sociology inevitably produces superstition pathology. We develop a disease or several diseases because we allow ourselves to cling to beliefs and practices born out of ignorance, and fear of the unknown. As humans, we are on a pathological behavioral trajectory of self-destruction. The separation that we have created is killing us. We are killing ourselves, other animals, and our planet. Many people can see it and feel it but don't know how to stop it.

Throughout the ages, from Tao Dao to Buddha, Jesus Christ, the Prophet Muhammad (s.a.w.s.), Mahatma Gandhi, Martin Luther King, Nelson Mandela, Mother Teresa and so many more, all taught the same fundamentals and life principles. If we look from within, there is only unconditional love and oneness. The only reason we look for love and belonging externally is because we have allowed ourselves to be consumed by fear and separateness. We are all inter-connected. Whether you look at it from a physical, intellectual, or spiritual perspective, they all lead to the same conclusion. Connection and oneness are all there is, and all there has ever been.

There are only two emotions: love and fear. Both require you to believe in something; however, they provide opposite results. Every other emotion we describe fits into either love or fear. Jealousy, anger, aggression, envy, manipulation, hate, judgment, and consequently the desire for war all come from fear. All our thoughts, our feelings, and our behaviors are influenced by whether we choose to come from a place of love or a place of fear. This choice is deeply rooted and resides at a subconscious level based on everything we have been taught and experienced in the past, as well as the generational experience we carry with us as part of our DNA.

Love in all its purity comes when we keep our hearts open regardless of the circumstance. With hearts open, we allow ourselves to feel the pain, yet express ourselves freely. It's only when we create separateness that we become fearful. When we operate from a place of fear, we separate ourselves from oneness, and as a result our behavior, our decisions, and our actions change.

How You See the World

I grew up seeing this all around me, and the only reason we have conflict is because of this separateness, greed, and the belief that for us to win, someone else must lose. We see this in everyday operations from business, to relationships, to world affairs. We can observe the division and the belief that to win it must be at all costs—a dog-eat-dog world! Even in organizations, we see so many departments working in what is known in the corporate world as "silos." A silo is like a business operating as separate businesses and in competition with each other even though they are part of the same company. They often seemingly operate against each other as if their survival depends on it. This creates a sense of lack and scarcity and so there must be a loser and a winner, losing sight of the fact that we are on the same team. We are all playing the game not to lose and if we keep focusing on not losing, all we will keep creating is more loss. Where your focus goes, your energy will flow.

In contrast, all the greats have witnessed, experienced, recognized, and taught that when we open our hearts and come from a place of unconditional love and oneness, there is abundance, and this is when we all win. It never has to be an "us or them" situation because the second you choose that notion, we all eventually lose. Every thought leads to a feeling, every feeling leads to an action, and every action has an equal reaction. And so, the cycle continues.

∾

Chapter 9

THE BIG LIE

How Fear Shapes Behavior and Decision-Making

"Absence of evidence is not evidence of absence."
-Edzard Ernst

I f we go back to the plight of the Jewish people, it is easy to understand their fears. Judaism's origins date back over 3,500 years and is one of the oldest religions. Judaism describes God as omnipresent and omnipotent. Over many years, their fear grew as a result of the expulsion of their ancestors, as well as the antisemitism they felt in the Middle East, Europe, and Great Britain. In the first half of the twentieth century, Jews were discriminated against in various areas around the world, including in the United States, and banned from working in some occupations. They could not rent or own certain properties, were not accepted as members of many social clubs, were not able to attend resort areas, and were banned from enrolling in colleges by quotas. Antisemitism reached its peak in the USA with the rise of the Ku Klux Klan in the 1920s. It wasn't until the end of World War II and the Holocaust that anti-Jewish sentiment drastically declined in the United States.

An Historical Context

The reason for their fear as a people is real and cannot be taken lightly. It is built into their DNA and has been constantly reaffirmed by history. We are dealing with generational trauma, and the impact it has had on people is enormous. As a people they are united, and they are strong from the outside in. Yet, at the same time, this can weaken them. Fear weakens us all. Fear closes us up, separates us, creates angst, worry, and self-doubt and has you constantly looking over your shoulder. Every event, every word, and every decision can create paranoia at a subconscious level, which leads people to make irrational decisions to protect themselves and their world, with little regard for anything or anyone outside of them. It leads people to an eventual path of self-destruction. That is what fear does to us all.

The modern Zionist movement played on this fear to keep their people united globally. It has become a case of us against the world at a very deep-rooted level to the point of extreme paranoia. The Israeli government plays on that fear with its citizens today. There are so many myths created about the Palestinians, Hamas, and other Arab nationalities that are repeated over and over for generations.

Even certain procedures have been created within the nation to keep fear alive. I am not saying these procedures were not necessary at some point, but imagine the fear it builds when these types of activities are repeated. As a child, I recall instances when Syrian planes were thought to be flying over the country. There would be army jeeps patrolling the streets, warning residents and encouraging them to go to the underground shelters. During the Gulf War, gas masks were promptly handed out to every Jewish Israeli citizen in case of a gas attack, which never happened.

Side note: the non-Jewish citizens of Israel (the Palestinians) were not given the gas masks initially until there was an outcry and pressure applied. Those Palestinians living in the occupied territories never received gas masks, even though it is Israel's duty as part of the

Geneva Convention rules and the protection of civilians under military occupation.

In 1948 as a new nation, military conscription became mandatory for eighteen-year-olds, both male and female, if they were Israeli Jews. Before they join the army, young Jews are taught about the Holocaust and how they are a special type of victim. By the time the child is eighteen, they are ready to fight the fight of the "good guys." It doesn't matter who the enemy is, those entering the army are ready to "protect and serve." According to Or Kashti in an article published in *Haaretz* (2017), a left-wing Israeli Jewish newspaper, "Israeli students undergo right-wing indoctrination before going on school trips abroad."

Learning Fear

"The messages are simple and repetitive," a mother of an eleventh-grade student from the central region says. "All the Arabs hate us, almost the entire world hates us." Noa Limone (Haaretz 2020) also wrote, "In Israel, indoctrination starts in kindergarten."

This type of indoctrination breeds fear in the form of hate from a young age. This tactic is not unique to Jewish Israelis. According to Human Rights Watch (Child Soldiers Global Report 2008), eighty-six countries recruit children under the age of eighteen. Indoctrination starts in childhood; for example, in Pakistan, suicide bombers ranged between the ages of twelve and eighteen. Between the years 2000 and 2008, there were cases of Palestinians involved in suicide bombing. This practice has ceased and since 2010, there have been no incidents reported. The point of this section is to say that if you repeat anything enough times to someone at some point, they will start to believe it at a core level. You do it over decades and longer through any means possible, and you can be assured it will stick, especially for young, impressionable children.

In order to clarify the way in which fear is used, let us first examine how the human mind works. According to 2005 research from the National Science Foundation, we have up to 60,000 thoughts per day. That figure can be as high as 90,000 thoughts per day. Of all those thoughts, 95% of them are repeated day in and day out. And if we are not careful, 80% of those repeated thoughts will be negative. So, if we are reinforcing the same messages day in and day out, we then create paradigms. Paradigms are formed from a multitude of habits that guide and govern every move you make. They affect the way you eat, the way you walk, and even the way you talk. They direct your communication, your work habits, your successes, and your failures. All these paradigms/habits reside in the subconscious mind. It is estimated 96% to 98% of your behavior is on autopilot because the brain is designed to help conserve energy. There are two ways we create these paradigms. The first is through constant, spaced repetition, and the second is through an event that has a considerable emotional impact.

Since we think in pictures, every single one of those thoughts we think each day creates an image on the screen of our mind. This image appears as if it were happening in the present tense. We dream in images in the present tense, we recall the past in images in the present tense, and, with a thought about the future, we even create events that have never happened, in an image as if it were happening right now. Our subconscious mind cannot differentiate between what is real and what is not. The second an image is created through thought—positive or negative—the subconscious mind believes it is true and that it is taking place right now, in the present. You keep repeating the same image(s) in the present tense, which then leads to your creating a paradigm, a story, and then a habit. Can you see where this is going?

We are repeating the same stories, creating the same fears, and designing our future based on past experiences. We subconsciously do this as individuals as well as on a global level. The result? We are creating our future from our familiar past and then wondering why we keep repeating the same mistakes, and never learn from them.

Big Lie Theory

The media and politics are masters at this, and you don't even realize you are being indoctrinated every time you turn the TV on, watch/read/listen to the news, watch various movies, or scroll through social media. It is also how advertising works—through subliminal messaging. It is said that on digital media, it takes eleven touch points to get the end user to react to a post, or action one of your requests. If you repeat something enough times, people will act on your post or advertising at some point without even realizing it.

In global affairs, this tactic has been used repeatedly regardless of whether the facts were true or not. It has come to be known as the "Big Lie Theory," which states, *"If you tell a lie big enough and keep repeating it, people will eventually come to believe it. The lie can be maintained only for such a time as the State can shield the people from the political, economic, and/or military consequences of the lie. It thus becomes vitally important for the State to use all of its powers to repress dissent, for the truth is the mortal enemy of the lie, and thus by extension, the truth is the greatest enemy of the State."*

This tactic was used by Hitler, the Israeli Government, ISIS, as well as Donald Trump, when it was suggested that he spent months spreading lies about the 2020 elections, which eventually may have resulted in the Capitol riots on January 6, 2021, among others.

Can you see why we need to ask questions and be willing to at least entertain new ideas before deciding to accept or reject them? This is pertinent to every part of our life. It's not always easy as we all have our paradigms and our own set of beliefs. But as human beings, we are here to grow. If we do not grow, if we do not evolve, we will disintegrate. Evolution is our singular purpose.

Stagnation and repeating history over and over again are killing us as a species, and we are killing the planet along with us. I am not talking about becoming a conspiracy theorist here, as that has its own problems. This is not about being "woke" either. This is simply about understanding the mechanics of the mind. We must override our habitual nature that is on autopilot; otherwise, we will keep repeating the same mistakes without ever fully examining them, and asking ourselves if this is the ultimate reality we want to create for the future of our children.

As soon as we are faced with an event, our mind goes searching through all the stored data from the past. There are billions and billions of bits of information stored at a subconscious level in the mind. Some are factual data, but a lot of it can be corrupt data. According to Joe Dispenza (2013 *Breaking the Habit of Being Yourself*), by the time we are thirty-five, up to 50% of our memories are made up. This is why there are no absolutes in arguments. When we feel ourselves being 100% adamant that we are right and someone else is wrong, we need to take a step back and ask ourselves, what is this based on? Is there anything I am not seeing? Could the other party be seeing it from another point of view? There is no right or wrong. There is perspective. If each of us is only aware of 2,000 bits of information in any given second out of 400 billion, could there perhaps be something we are not seeing? Could there be a different perspective to consider? Wayne Dyer said it best, *"When you change the way you look at things, the things you look at change."*

A Different Choice

We need to consciously choose either factual data or create a new set of data. When we choose corrupt data, it can lead to all sorts of issues because the data you choose will determine the type of truth from which you are operating. Ask yourself, "Am I choosing to work with the imagined truth, the apparent truth, or the ultimate truth? What evidence do I have to support my truth? What assumption am I making behind this truth?" And finally, one of the most powerful questions: "What do I want to believe?" The assumption behind your belief forms your belief.

Your beliefs form your thoughts, which then influence your emotions at a subconscious level. The ancient Greeks referred to the subconscious mind as the heart. Our body is nothing more than an instrument of the subconscious mind, and we react based on our emotions and feelings, thereby shaping our behavior, which in turn creates our experience and then our reality. If you go back to the beginning, if you choose to accept corrupt data, then your reality will be distorted. This is why it is so critical to keep ourselves open to questions.

The intention of questioning everything is not to come from a place of judgment or self-deprecation, but rather from a place of curiosity, a desire to learn, to serve and grow. By asking questions of ourselves and being open to receiving a different viewpoint, we become consciously aware of our fears, paradigms, and things that are holding us back. We need to see this as a gift and not try to protect ourselves by closing our hearts and building barriers. It's then that we begin to make decisions that benefit everyone. We start to play the game to win rather than playing the game **not** to lose. We have the belonging equation back to front. We don't actually need to look for belonging and approval, because we already have both.

Challenging Misconceptions

The last time I walked down the streets of my old country, I could feel the tension and fear everywhere. I remember an incident, many years ago, at an Ulpan (Hebrew language Centre) in Haifa I was attending to re-learn Hebrew. I had been studying daily for two and a half weeks at this center with a lot of new Jewish immigrants. Most of these new immigrants were from America and most assumed I was a new immigrant from Australia. One fellow student from New York had followed his Israeli-Jewish girlfriend and was learning Hebrew anew. We had some recordings to do as part of our homework and he had his girlfriend listen to my recordings; she was impressed with my accent in Hebrew for someone who was so "new" to the country. At lunch times the whole class would sit together and discuss various topics, and during this time the topic of "Arabs" only came up once when a couple of the students, who were married, mentioned they would be living in a beautiful newly established settlement in the occupied territories after they finish from the Ulpan. The husband mentioned how excited they were, except that their settlement would be surrounded by the "dirty" Arabs.

Having been in the class daily for over two weeks, no one had asked me a question. I realized they did not know I was one of those Arabs (remember, we are referred to as Arab Israelis and not Palestinians in the 1948 borders of the newly formed State of Israel). Later that week, the teacher asked several questions in class to determine everyone's status. She asked those students who were returned Jews to put their hands up. She then asked those who were "making Aliyah" to raise their hand. She finally asked the Arab Jews who had lived in other parts of the Middle East to raise theirs. That's when I realized she was referring to me. When I did not put my hand up for any of the questions, she looked at me curiously and asked why I had not raised my hand. I smiled and responded, "I was born and raised in Haifa; my entire family has always lived here, and I am an Arab." This startled her as she let out a gasp and proclaimed in surprise, "You are an Arab?" She had assumed I was a Jew originally from Tunisia or something similar. She did collect herself quickly and mentioned that she had been learning Arabic, but this episode left most of my classmates shocked and bewildered. It was only my New York friend who smiled, knowingly. Most of those sitting in the class were startled. They had not been so closely acquainted with a Palestinian before. A lot of what they thought they knew about us would have beem dispelled because they came to know and accept me as one of them. Ultimately, it was a great lesson in perception and preconceived ideas.

The truth is, there is no such thing as a winner or a loser. All I see is everyone losing, and until we understand this, there will be suffering for all involved and there will never be peace for anyone. When you oppress another, you will always live in fear that they may turn around and do the same to you.

In essence, there is no rest for the oppressed or the oppressor. Eventually, it will also impact every country globally as we sit back, watch, and deceive ourselves into thinking that it will not reach our own shores. The Palestinian issue is, in fact, a humanitarian crisis, not a Middle Eastern conflict.

My biggest observation to date when it comes to the question of the newly formed country of Israel and the Jewish fear is this: throughout history, as a result of fear and the constant spaced repetition of the same thoughts, they are creating the same separation and repeating the same damaging history.

As for Palestinians, they have no intention of leaving their lands or dreams behind. The objective of Ben-Gurion, the first Israeli Prime Minister, was to move villages and cities of the Indigenous people out of the country in hopes that they would eventually either die off or forget about their plight as the new generations came through. Unfortunately for him and others, this simply hasn't happened. Why? Because, just like the Jewish people, Palestinians have their own paradigms and beliefs that have formed over generations. We must remember that for as far back as history goes, non-Jewish Palestinians (their ancestors) resided on the same land and had to deal with the same wars, invasions, and suffering. They too are Semitic, and the notion of antisemitism as pertaining to be anti-Jewish originated in the Western World. Palestinians have never been and never will be antisemitic. It goes against their nature. The only difference is that in the Palestinian psyche, throughout the ages while they experienced pain and destruction, they believe they have outlived every single invader and conqueror, no matter what the consequences have been.

Even without an army and strong leadership, they have outlived and out-survived every single interloper, and view the latest colonizer and invader just the same as those who arrived before them. The modern state of Israel in the Palestinian mind is merely another one of the many occupiers over the ages. While its brutality has been severe, Palestinians believe at their core that they will outlive this as well—just like they have every other occupier.

We know where attention goes, energy flows, and the repeated images we create on the screen of our mind are what we create in reality. This is the same for collective consciousness and energy. So, the question then becomes, what is Zionism creating for itself? If Zionists constantly focus on their past suffering, and separate themselves from the world, keeping all others at arm's length, are they merely creating more suffering for themselves and others? Is history repeating itself? Palestinians in their heart of hearts believe that "this too shall pass," regardless of the current pain caused and the injustices which the world is at present turning a blind eye to. So, you can see where their attention and energy are going and what is being created?

Zionism, on the other hand, is built on fear and lack. While it may seem to have a global stronghold at present, it has many flaws and weaknesses. The more desperate a regime is, the more punitive it becomes. Eventually, this desperation will lead to self-destruction. We are seeing that today with hundreds of thousands of Israeli Jews in Tel Aviv protesting the government's proposal to change the judiciary system. The protesters see this as a threat to their democracy. In truth, how can there be a claim that Israel was founded on a true democracy when we see the segregation and oppression of Palestinians in the occupied territories and Israel?

Democracy rests on the premise that it includes all people. If the foundation is not based on this truth, then the foundations will eventually collapse. What the consequences are for the existence of the Israeli regime and the Jewish people through this self-destructive behavior, only time will tell. Because this is no longer a local issue, it begs the question: if this Zionist behavior is leading to self-destruction, what impact is it going to have on the entire world given its global reach and power?

This translates easily into our everyday life. Long-term, the way behavior manifests itself will impact everyone when we are operating from a place of fear. You may feel like you are winning short-term through power, manipulation, backstabbing, and looking after self-centered outcomes, but long-term it will come back to hurt you. In Australia this is known as the boomerang effect—once you throw it out, it must come back to you!

Choosing unconditional love may feel like the road less traveled, but ultimately, over time, it always wins. Unconditional love is not weak, and it's not just a bunch of "woo-woo." It takes inner courage and strength to keep your heart open and allow yourself to feel the pain yet choose to *"love your enemies and pray for those who perse-cute you."* This message was handed down to us over 2,000 years ago during the *Sermon on the Mount* and is said to be one of the most important sermons to this day.

Nelson Mandela spent the first eighteen of his twenty-seven years in jail at the brutal Robben Island prison. It took him going to one of the harshest jails in the world to realize the answer is uncondi-tional love: *"If you want to make peace with your enemy, you have to work with your enemy. Then he becomes your partner."* He set about demonstrating this one single piece of truth to bring an end to apartheid in South Africa.

We know the balance of power and leadership comes and goes. Everything has a beginning and an end, with no exceptions, so just ask yourself what legacy you want to leave. What impact do you want to have on your world and subsequently, the whole world?

Let's go back to our understanding of what we are thinking, and how we are feeling. Given that 96 to 98% of our behavior operates at a subconscious level, we must become self-aware of every thought we have. If you can imagine an iceberg, under the surface of the water, on one side we have love, and on the other side fear. At any given point, you can only choose to operate from a place of one or the other. Above the surface is the behavior that you see manifesting because of the emotion you choose to engage with. The quicker you understand this within yourself, the quicker you will recognize it in others. You will then know how to deal with it from a place of understanding.

The more you understand your behavior, the better you will understand others' behavior. Most people will look at others first to avoid the pain it may cause if they study themselves.

Take time out to become self-aware and to study yourself—become a student of self! Welcome and allow the truth as well as the pain to the surface; open your heart, and in doing so observe how the pain dissolves. The only reason we turn pain into suffering is because we suppress the feelings instead of expressing them. This causes us to allow ourselves to live in fear at a subconscious level, which manifests in all sorts of "self-protective" and "unproductive" behavior. Again, above the surface, depending on which emotion you choose to operate from, the observable behavior will manifest.

EMOTIONAL MANAGEMENT

THE ICEBERG

GRATITUDE TO ONESELF & OTHERS	AGGRESSION
GIVING TO ONESELF & OTHERS	ANGER
COOPERATION	DEPRESSION
UNDERSTANDING	PROCRASTINATION
FUNNY	MANIPULATION

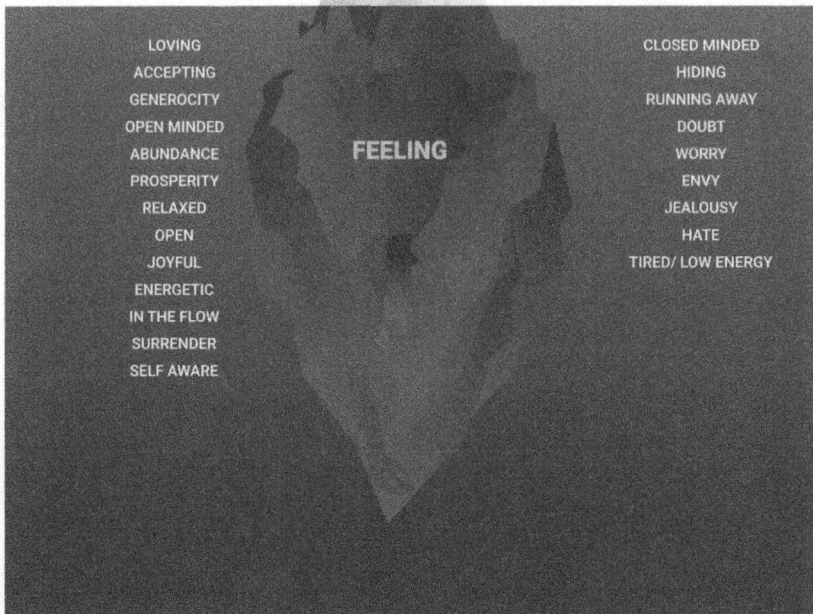

BEHAVIOUR

LOVING	CLOSED MINDED
ACCEPTING	HIDING
GENEROCITY	RUNNING AWAY
OPEN MINDED	DOUBT
ABUNDANCE	WORRY
PROSPERITY	ENVY
RELAXED	JEALOUSY
OPEN	HATE
JOYFUL	TIRED/ LOW ENERGY
ENERGETIC	
IN THE FLOW	
SURRENDER	
SELF AWARE	

FEELING

UNCONDITIONAL LOVE	FEAR
Joyful	Melancholic
Giving to oneself and others	Jealous
Grateful to oneself and others	Resentful
Cooperative	Envious
Understanding of oneself and others	Manipulative
Open	Low on energy
Adventurous	Blaming
Restful	Anxious
Funny	Humourless
Creative	Closed Minded
In the flow	Scared
Relaxed	Stressed
Energetic	Worried
Caring	Procrastinating
Kind to oneself and others	Perfectionist
Abundant	Addicted
Prosperous	Lacking
Loving oneself and others	Aggressive
Accepting oneself and others	Judgemental

Be guided by your feelings. If you are not feeling good, if you are feeling weak, sad, scared, or angry then it is coming from a place of fear. The easiest and first question to ask yourself when you are in this situation and must decide is, "Is this coming from a place of fear, or love?"

Have a look at the table above, or the iceberg diagram and pinpoint your feelings. Just be open to entertaining new ideas when you are in this place. You have nothing to lose and everything to gain. If you can see this is coming from a place of fear, then ask yourself more questions. Don't expect yourself to change immediately but do allow yourself to feel the feelings. Entertain the questions and sit with them for a while in stillness, as Jesus did for forty days and nights and as Nelson Mandela did in solitary confinement. (You need not ruminate on it for long.) Over time you will find yourself shifting towards love, because that is our natural place to be, and it is a lot easier to love than to fear. We have an abundant amount of energy for love and a very limited amount for fear. That's why when we are aligned with our true purpose, we have so much energy and when we are not aligned, we hear ourselves telling everyone how tired we are.

Some of the questions to ponder and ask yourself include:

- Is this what I want to believe?
- How else can I look at this?
- What am I not seeing?
- Who can help me see it more clearly?
- What if it could be easy?
- What evidence do I have to prove this?
- How do I want to feel?
- What if I could do it?
- What do I want?
- Where is this coming from? Love or Fear?
- What is my behavior telling me?
- What are my feelings telling me?
- Am I coming from a position of inner strength or inner weakness?
- Am I being the hero of my own story or the victim?

- What do I want to do with this information?
- Who do I choose to be with regard to this situation?

Conscious awareness of our feelings will determine our behavior. How we react will be the game changer for you, me, and the world in all areas. We must always come from a position of inner strength, not from a position of weakness and fear. We cannot be both the hero and the victim of our own story. In other words, no matter what life throws at you, no matter how hard things get, rise above it, and don't ever play the victim.

It doesn't mean we won't feel pain, loss, and sorrow. Through rejection, heartbreak, divorce, loss of a loved one, manipulation, unforeseen circumstances, and barriers, there will be hard times and we will fall. We will feel pain. Pain is inevitable, it's suffering that's the choice! (Buddha). Scars heal and wounds mend, and you can use them to make yourself stronger.

If you want to live freely, find true love, be successful, have the quality of life you dream of, and live in prosperity, joy, and abundance devoid of suffering, then ask yourself one further question: "What would unconditional love do?"

This is the single most powerful question you can ask yourself...go deep within and open your heart. Every decision you make from there will be the right decision. Will you choose unconditional love, or will it be fear that guides your decisions and behavior?

Unconditional love is the most powerful force ever created. It will not make you weak or a pushover; it will rid you of fear. Without fear, you will take everything and everyone into account, including yourself. You realize we are all connected and one. The truth is, you can have it all; you just need to believe you can, and then choose to follow that path regardless of the circumstances and pressure around you, with calmness of mind and laser-like focus.

〜

Chapter 10

THE SOLUTION

Exploring Interconnectedness

"Be the change you want to see in this world."
- Mahatma Gandhi

T he real solution for all of us is to go back to the source of the separation theory and change our mindset. Separation is an illusion, as we separated ourselves from God. This reminds me of a story Buddha shared with his followers, teaching them about the illusory nature of separation.

"Once, in a dense forest, there were four blind men who had never seen an elephant before. They were curious about this magnificent creature, so they decided to visit a nearby village where an elephant resided, to learn about it. The villagers led the blind men to the elephant and allowed them to touch and feel the animal so they could understand its true nature.

The first blind man touched the elephant's side and said, "An elephant is like a great, sturdy wall." The second blind man felt the elephant's tusk and declared, "No, an elephant is like a sharp, pointed spear." The third blind man grasped the elephant's trunk, and he was certain that the elephant resembled a thick, writhing snake. Finally, the fourth blind man touched the elephant's leg and proclaimed, "You are all wrong. An elephant is like a strong, tall tree."

Each of the blind men believed that their individual experience and understanding of the elephant represented the whole truth. They argued and insisted that their perspective was the only correct one. The villagers, who could see the entire elephant, recognized that each of the blind men was only partially right. In reality, the elephant was much greater and more complex than any one of them could perceive.

Buddha then went on to explain, "Just like the blind men and the elephant, people often perceive only a fragment of reality while believing that their limited understanding represents the entire truth. They cling to their separate experiences, failing to recognize that everything in the world is interconnected, and any notion of separation is an illusion."

Buddha taught his followers about the interconnectedness of all things and the dangers of clinging to the false belief in separation. Similarly, differing religious institutions believed that God is somewhere over there, and we are all over here, and they also decided that God was a man based on the image of ourselves. If God can punish us and have vengeful tendencies if we do not obey his word, then what chance do we have of treating each other any differently? We have permitted ourselves to fight, kill, and be vengeful because we modeled our behavior on the version of God that we built.

Identity Based on Separation

The world is entrenched in the belief of separation, and we don't question it because we fear losing our individuation. "Who am I if I am not a Palestinian, an American, or an Israeli Jew, etc.?" we ask ourselves. "If we are one, then we will lose our individuality," we think to ourselves. Look at the fingers on your hand, though; they are not separate, yet they are individual, and each one has a function. No two snowflakes are alike, yet they all come from one source.

"You are not a drop in the ocean, you are the ocean in a drop."

— *Rumi*

What about waves? While each wave is a part of the ocean, it is a separate entity in and of itself. No two souls are alike, yet no soul is separate from the higher power. From the very beginning, our oneness and unity were all-inclusive.

God never produces anything separately. Perhaps it is way past time to upgrade our beliefs and definition of God. Jesus Christ came to assist humanity in evolving with love and compassion, and he was crucified for it. So, what we are discussing here is not new, but the time has come to open our minds and hearts to accept that we are all one.

We are all searching for belonging and unity, yet it is impossible to find what has never been lost. We need to have a hard look at ourselves in the mirror and express who we are. Why keep denying what we are? Why do we keep refusing to accept this? Is it because we confuse oneness with sameness?

Are we afraid all 400 faiths will become one? And if this were to happen, which faith would we have to choose? Will we need to go to war over it again? Do we need to be reminded of all the wars throughout history, caused by religious beliefs? And, what about the end-of-days prophecy—the one-world religion described in Revelation 17:1–18 as "the great harlot?" Is this where we are heading if we chose one religion?

Seeing the Full Picture

To answer these questions, we need to look back at where conflict originated. The conflict originated from the first idea we created on separateness.

The original sin was not when Adam and Eve ignored what God had said by eating the forbidden fruit. The original sin was when we chose to see ourselves as separate from God and place him away from us, up in the clouds, and supposedly out of our reach. We have been paying the price ever since.

It does not have to be this way. What if oneness allowed for individual differences and uniqueness? What if we can agree on oneness and keep all of our faiths? Why do we have to choose one faith over another? We have so much to learn from all faiths and there is beauty in all of them.

Have you ever gone to a mosque and taken part in prayers? Have you ever been in a synagogue and participated? What about a Buddhist temple or an Aboriginal ceremony? Try it out one day.

There is much beauty in all of these experiences, and each one is a spiritual experience that helps us grow. So back to the question: what if we could agree that we are all connected, and all originate from one source? This is the whole point of tolerance and acceptance, which helps us to keep our individuality. Would that change the way we view things?

The Impact of One on the Whole

All we need is to change our cultural story. What I do for you, I do for me. What affects you, affects me. Once the first domino falls, the rest will follow. We need to change that first domino. So, the question becomes, "Am I willing to be the first domino?"

If you want something, give what you want to another. This is one of the most powerful concepts we have at our disposal. Think about it, you cannot give something you do not have. The more you give of what you want, the more of it you will have. If you want more love, give more love unconditionally. If you want more money, give money to others. This applies to everything.

Practice this daily and work on it consciously. What you give to others, you give to yourself because of our oneness. Oneness is not sameness, and it is not weakness. All the masters since the dawn of time understood this truth. Their power did not come from their sword, but rather from their heart.

There are reports that when Nelson Mandela was released after twenty-seven years, his jailers wept. When asked by the reporters why they wept, they said they had lost their best friend. Once, he was considered a terrorist and one of the most dangerous men by his jailers, the police, and the South African government as led by the National Party. Now, he is known as the man who changed the nation through his policy of reconciliation and healing, which lifted the country many feared would fall into a racial war. It is from solitude and quietness that all our answers, and ultimate truth will come.

On the flip side, as we can see today, if you give hate, you will get hate. If you oppress others, you will always look over your shoulder in fear of retribution. If you deny people their freedom, you will never have your own freedom.

Jesus said, "Do unto others as you will have done unto you." This is how we break the cycle.

One of the most powerful questions Neale Donald Walsch asks is, "What hurts you so bad that makes you feel you have to do what you did to me in order to heal it?" Imagine what impact this one single question would have on Israeli/Zionist Jews, Palestinians, or any other contentious situation in the world. Imagine if you approached every conflict you have with this question. This is the approach Nelson Mandela took with his jailers and oppressors.

You may be wondering: How can we be so forgiving, given the atrocities and crimes against humanity are still going on today? How, as Palestinians, are they going to be so forgiving? Or how could the Jewish people be so forgiving of all that they have had to endure?

This is not about forgiving people, as one could argue there is nothing to forgive. When you understand what is driving people's behavior, forgiveness is not needed.

Every ill treatment comes from fear. Greed comes from fear as does control, and the exertion of undue power on others. God understands oneness, but we as humans are still so primitive that it remains at times difficult to comprehend. Understanding and compassion replace forgiveness in the eyes of the master, which means, we, too, can be understanding, as we are all created in the image of God and therefore, not separated.

Compassion Transforms the World

Understanding, however, does not mean we let go of our principles and values. We can understand, not by abandoning our principles, but by putting ourselves in a place where we realize the other side has gone through the same thing. No one does anything inappropriate based on their view of their world. Perception is a very powerful thing. Change what you believe to be true, change the assumptions you make behind the belief, and you will be able to change your behavior. Change the model of the world and you change the behavior.

> *"You never change things by fighting the existing reality.*
> *To change something, build a new model that*
> *makes the existing model obsolete."*

> — *R. Buckminster Fuller*

Seeing With Your Heart

As Neale Donald Walsch also asks, "Is it possible that there is something we don't fully understand here? Is there something we don't understand about God or life?" We think we understand it all, but we don't.

At this point, take a few minutes alone and ask yourself, "Who do I think other people are?" Sit with this question in silence and contemplate it.

It's time that each one of us, should we choose to, becomes the source rather than the seeker of answers. Quiet your mind and spend some time alone. The length of time will depend on you, and you can do it intermittently. There are no rules, but we know how important it is to be in solitude so as to be one with the source. Jesus did that for forty days and forty nights in preparation for his mission. It was in twenty-seven years of solitude that Nelson Mandela found the truth.

Be the Source of Love

Solitude is the key to higher self-awareness. It's where we can think and reflect to see the same things with new eyes. It's where many of the magical experiences happen. It's when you are alone that you feel the most love. Do you know why this is? Do you think it may be because we are all connected, and we will always feel love no matter where we are or what we are doing?

Even the seemingly harshest of people on the outside want to feel a sense of belonging, and they are moved by love. We see something on TV that is so moving it can make the strongest person cry. Why is that? Because, as we are watching, we switch off the logical brain and the intellect, whilst the heart automatically takes over, and it knows nothing but love.

You may ask: How can I be the source? Who will I be the source for? I am not like the masters. Who do I think I am? Well, here it is in a nutshell: no one can do you as well as you do you. No one!

People fear oneness because they believe it brings the loss of individuality and their identifying point of difference. However, nothing could be further from the truth. This point, too, cannot be repeated enough. Being connected does not mean being the same, nor does it mean that life has to be nondescript and boring. We can instead celebrate all our nationalities, faiths, and cultural richness with joy and excitement as we explore the wonderful and intricate tapestry of contrasting cultures, cuisines, traditions, and languages.

No two souls are the same, just like no two fingerprints are the same.

What we must do is learn to accept, love, respect, cherish and enjoy the richness of our differences, while understanding the connection we all have, and that every single difference is all part of the universal ecosystem, that is oneness.

To be the source means you stop playing the game "not to lose," and you start to realize that you do have the answers and there are things you can do. You stop comparing yourself to others and think there is no way you can be as great as the great teachers because you start to realize that you are one with them. If you allow yourself, you will begin to realize you have been gifted with more talent and ability than you can ever hope to use in your lifetime. Your only duty is to use that talent and ability to give back and serve.

Rather than allowing your intellect to ask, "Who do I think I am to see myself as the source?," **allow your heart to ask:**

- Who do I think I am *not* to share my gifts with the world?
- What are the consequences of playing small and *not* sharing my soul's purpose in this world?
- Who do I think I am to think I am *not* that great?
- Who do I think I am *not*?
- What impact does holding back my true purpose and potential have on my life and those around me?
- What right do I have to allow myself to deny my soul's purpose in life?

We live simultaneously on three levels:

1. As **spiritual** beings or souls
2. By means of the **intellect** with the spectacular mind
3. Physically through the wonderful **body** with which we were born

We are all here to have this physical experience called "life." Through the physical experience, we create a separation just like a wave does with the ocean. We come from one, rise up still connected but as individuals, and then blend back into the oneness. Just as a wave goes back into the ocean as one, at the end of our physical life we go back to where we came from.

While we are in our physical experience, we are here to take delight in life in all its glory and with as much joy as possible. Some of the biggest questions that humankind has ever asked of itself and continues to ask are, "What is the meaning of life?" and "What is my purpose?" or "What is all this about?"

Our one true purpose is to grow and evolve. It is to touch lightly and find our joy. It is to connect to our soul's purpose and live from the inside out. It is to find calmness of mind to share our gifts and enjoy the love.

The physical plane on which we live, or more simply put, the physical body that we live in, is nothing more than an instrument of our beautiful, spectacular mind. Our body will react or respond according to what we are thinking and how we are feeling. The results in our life that we experience and how we view life will all depend on what we choose to think and feel.

This may sound simple. That's because it is.

With Your Head and With Your Heart

When you hear or read of people professing "you are what you think," or "thoughts become things," that is exactly what is happening. We are masters at manifesting and creating, and as such we do not need lessons in the art of manifestation. With every thought and every feeling, we are creating our reality on a moment-by-moment basis. Isn't it incredible to know you are the captain of your own ship called life, and anything you can imagine, then believe as true, you can ultimately achieve? The biggest question we have to go back to is, what are we creating and why do we continue to create things that we do not want individually, or collectively?

To delve deeper into this creation of separateness, let's look at the first and second planes on which we operate: the *intellectual* and the *spiritual*, or in other words, the *soul*. The mind at an intellectual level is a marvelous, miraculous, beautiful tool, but it is secondary to the heart. The heart is our gateway to the soul. It is the central chakra that provides the balance and the connection to oneness. It is the Source when we tap into it. There is nothing you need when you go to the Source.

The intellect, or the head, is a true gift for us all, and there is a fine balance in the connection between the heart and the head. The head is our consciousness, and it is separate from the heart. We do not have to educate the heart. The heart educates us, and it is the link between the spirit and the body.

My Aunt Khazni, may she rest in peace, was not an educated woman and could not read or write, but she knew so much about life, and the heart. I spent a lot of time at her home while she was in the kitchen preparing meals, and she would always say, "Reem, never close your heart," as she clenched her hand tightly shut to demonstrate, "Always keep it wide open," as she gently opened wide the palm of her hand. "Keeping your heart open will teach you so much about people and you will feel their pain. This is how you will learn to treat everyone, including yourself, with respect and dignity."[1]

In stillness, we can tap into the heart and, therefore, the soul and the source. "Be still, and know I am God" has been practiced through the ages. When you quiet the world outside of you and turn off your senses (which were designed to help you navigate through your physical world), you will begin to tap into your heart and, therefore, your soul. In stillness, you can hear the quiet and peaceful inner voice that will lead you to all the wisdom and answers of the universe.

The intellect is truly a gift, yet it has become our stumbling block as it searches for ways to create differences. If allowed to, the intellect will create chaos, and people become accustomed to operating in this chaos. Overthinking can create chaos. When you are faced with a challenging decision or a stressful situation, you may begin to over-analyze the possible outcomes, causing a whirlwind of thoughts and emotions. This overthinking can lead to anxiety, indecision, and even paralysis, as you struggle to decide the best course of action. The action we choose to take can have a serious impact on productivity, damage relationships, and affect our mental health.

The intellect cannot be still, and its main purpose is to constantly inquire and find its own type of sense. The intellect looks for differences, which puts it in conflict with the heart, which seeks only unity and love.

Do you know why we allow chaos to rule? We have allowed our senses (sight, hearing, touch, smell, and taste) to actually rule our lives rather than merely being the tools that we use to help us navigate our physical world. We have allowed ourselves to constantly react to the external circumstances that our senses pick up, rather than respond to them to help us navigate the journey to reach our goal.

We have allowed the mind to become the master, and relegated the heart to be secondary to the mind. We have allowed our 60,000 to 90,000 thoughts per day, which will be mostly negative if we do not monitor them, to be repeated day in and day out. These repeated thoughts control how we feel, and we make decisions accordingly. The vast majority of us have turned this beautiful gift we have been given into our biggest obstacle. If there is no tangible difference, then our intellect seeks to create one, and consequently, will go searching for a sense of belonging from elements of the outside world.

To be Kind or Right

How do we begin to turn this around? We have to practice and learn to abide by the heart. When we turn the heart into the master, we then automatically turn the mind or intellect into the intelligent servant.

This is where it's important to consider what unconditional love would guide us to do. In any given situation, you can stop and find a moment of silence to ask yourself, "At a core level, am I love or am I fear/hate/jealousy/resentment, etc.?" Then, allow that answer to guide your next decision.

Whenever I feel my own heart tighten and recognize that I am either judging, comparing, being jealous, or feeling fearful in a given situation, I ask myself, "Who am I at a core level? Do I want to hate my enemy? Do I want to argue knowing full well that I will not be able to convince others of my point of view? Or do I want to understand the others' position and point of view before I move forward from a place of love, and an open heart?" It's not always easy, but which is better: to be kind, or right? And even if I am right, how have I been part of a fair solution?

Imagine if each of us embraced these questions. We would see an end to family rifts, major arguments, and disagreements, fighting, racism, oppression, and our self-destructive behavior on a day-to-day basis, at an individual level as well as on a global scale.

Most people at this stage would argue that this is simply not possible because things happen daily that make it impossible to end arguments, misunderstandings, and conflicts. It would take every single person to live like the masters, and there is no such thing as a perfect world.

There is truth to that thinking. Life is messy, and there will always be situations and events that challenge us. Furthermore, our journey in life is never going to be smooth sailing. However, this is what creates contrast in our lives, allowing us to see and experience what we do not want in life, only to realize what it is we do actually want.

By the law of nature, everything has a polar opposite. If there is good, there must be bad. Since we have the darkness of the night, then consequently we also experience the brightness of the day. Where there is an up, there must be a down. Joy comes hand in hand with pain. To feel and experience joy, achievement, love, accomplishment, success, etc. we must know what the opposite feels like. How can you possibly recognize and appreciate the positive if you don't know what the negative feels like?

The entire purpose of our physical existence on Earth is to experience joy, happiness, and love. Yet, seemingly negative situations also play a pivotal role in our lives. Most people live their lives trying to avoid the perceived negative contrast at all costs. However, ironically, the more we try to resist that which we do not want, the more suffering and hardship we create for ourselves.

Struggle as a Catalyst

What if we were to change our definition of this contrast? What if we stop seeing it as something negative, and instead embrace contrasting experiences as an opportunity to identify that which we do not want, thereby bringing us closer to understanding that which we actually do desire? Or, what if we were to see it as a learning opportunity, providing us with the growth that we need to move us closer to the goals we wish to achieve?

Sit with this concept for a little while and think about it. Think about every single one of your own experiences you have had which you had perhaps defined as being negative—are there any that led to bigger and better things? Would you then look back and acknowledge that if that one bad thing had not happened, you might not actually be where you are today? Have you ever been broken-hearted, only to find your true love at some point in the future? Have you ever been rejected for a promotion or a job, only to land a much more desirable role a little while later? How does it feel when you finally achieve what you want? It's pretty sweet, isn't it? It feels incredible when you overcome adversity, doesn't it? You then realize how strong you have become, how capable you are and how much that element of contrast is needed for you to progress in your journey. In such instances, therefore, should we not embrace this contrast, or the supposed unwanted situation, knowing in full faith that the ultimate win will be so much more rewarding?

The question is not whether we have failures, or if our journey through life will be a bumpy one given that it is a near certainty each and every one of us will fail countless times throughout our lives. Anyone who has ever achieved anything of any significance has had failures and experienced some form of pain. The question is, how long do you want to wallow in pain and turn it into suffering?

Mindful Recalibration

When we turn pain into suffering, it means we have closed our hearts, and we have separated ourselves from everything around us. It's also not a question of "How will I continue to be calm and never get angry, sad, mad, envious, jealous, fearful, or upset, etc.?" That is an impossible task. The questions are: "How quickly can I recognize the state I am in and turn it around through acceptance and understanding?" "How quickly can I reopen my heart?" "How quickly can I remember to ask myself, 'what would unconditional love do in this situation?'" and "How quickly can I recalibrate and respond to the situation, rather than react?"

The journey of life, from the second you start it until the second it is over, is about peaks and valleys, ups and downs. So, ask yourself: How can I possibly avoid the low points if they are an inevitable part of life? How do I redefine my relationship with the difficult times in life? What energy do I give it when I am experiencing a so-called valley in life, and is there a different way I can look at it?

No one in the world has ever been able to completely avoid life's low points or challenges, and it would be extremely beneficial if we were taught this from a young age. The most beautiful gift we can give our children is the gift of unconditional love and resilience, thereby providing strong foundations upon which the best leadership frameworks can be built. The most adept leaders and masters in the world understand this one concept as if it were ingrained in their DNA.

It's not that these leaders and masters never experienced the contrast in life. Of course they did. They, too, experienced anger, felt discouraged, and probably questioned their paths in life. With practice, though, they understood the need to accept these feelings and situations so as to move into a place of unconditional love and resilience. They could quickly redefine the situation and get back on track with laser-like focus, regardless of the circumstances.

Even Jesus himself experienced an entire gamut of emotions during his life—from the joy of following his ultimate goal and leading people in love, to anger at the hypocrisy of the religious elite whose hardened hearts meant that they showed no remorse in oppressing the less privileged. He showed a love of all people, regardless of their ethnicity and religious background, and he experienced sorrow as he brought Lazarus back from death. He had compassion for all, regardless of their way of life. Nonetheless, he also felt disgust at the greed and oppression of the poor in the temple, and the Court of the Gentiles, when money laundering and price-fixing prevented the non-Jewish people from honoring God with sacrifices. He experienced belief with absolute clarity (which we still feel the effects of over 2,000 years later) as well as doubt and despair as he asked the question, "My God, my God, why hast thou forsaken me?" And he experienced highs and lows, from the endless supply of energy to heal the ill and weak, to exhaustion and understanding that he needed to retreat from people and reconnect with God alone and in peace.

Lessons and Gifts from Adversity

Some of my earliest lessons to be learned from adversity came when we lived in Haifa and my mother worked in Nazareth with people from all communities, religions, and ethnic backgrounds. I had this incredible opportunity to meet and befriend amazing people who had overcome so many hardships in life. We had close family members who had been imprisoned for "political" reasons. So, we'd spend weekends visiting prisons. There, we were treated like cattle in gated metal pens by the guards while awaiting our turn in line. These memories taught me so much, but I will share more about that later.

Where my mother was teaching, I also had the opportunity to meet young children who had lost limbs and eyesight from explosions. There was one boy I remember spending time with at Mum's school in Nazareth who had lost his eyesight, skin around his head, one arm, and a leg from the knee down. He had been innocently playing football in the fields when he was gravely wounded by a "shiny" ball he had come across. His name was Muhammad and he came from a nearby village. Despite Muhammad's obvious physical disabilities, he was one of the smartest kids academically, played football like a pro, and was musically gifted in playing the Durbaki (the traditional Palestinian drum). Muhammad helped shape my attitude towards adversity for the rest of my life. I learned there and then that we are defined by our adversity, and how we allow adversity to define us is our choice.

Mohammad never saw himself as a victim, despite what he had been through with the bomb that nearly killed him—a bomb that had been placed by the army where children play. When I was young, I spoke to my mum about this. She said to me, "Reem, no matter what happens to you in life, always come from a position of strength, and never from a position of weakness." In other words, no matter what life throws at you, no matter how hard things get, rise above it and don't play the victim. This memory, being my first lesson in leadership, has been etched into my subconscious mind for life.

It doesn't mean we won't feel pain, loss, and sorrow. Through rejection, heartbreak, divorce, loss of a loved one, manipulation, unforeseen circumstances, and barriers, there will of course be hard times, and we will fall. We will feel pain.

When we fall, it becomes a question of: What role do you want to play in it? How do you want adversity to define you? And how long will it take to pick yourself up and make it count?

The journey from where you are today to where you want to be is the ebb and flow of life. That is what we call life—our journey, and our learning, if we choose it to be such. Again, we need to remember that you cannot be the victim and the hero in your own story at the same time. You must choose one or the other. Which will you choose?

～

Chapter 11

THE CHOICE

Roles of Victim or Hero

O n a level of mass consciousness, choosing to play the victim or the hero of our story has a significant impact on us all, globally. We watch as nations simultaneously try to assume the role of both the "victim and the hero," something which, in and of itself, is untenable. You cannot be the victim *and* the hero in the same story. You must make a choice.

Playing the Victim and the Hero

When we look at the past and keep repeating our mistakes rather than learning from them, we are allowing fear and ego to dictate our next move. We play the role of the victim without even realizing it, all the while thinking we are being strong. We allow fear to set into our cultural psyche whenever the oppressed becomes the oppressor, or when we believe the only way to win is for someone else to lose. It makes us believe that we must protect ourselves at all costs. Here we are inadvertently playing the blame game and the victim card. Interestingly enough, it is also when you hear people and nations justifying the unjustifiable.

When a nation with so much power plays the victim card, real problems and ramifications can be expected. This is not an easy concept to explain, knowing that what I share has the potential to offend and cause many people to take exception. Please know that this is coming from a place of understanding and love, not from a place of judgment. How else are we going to reach a position of mutual understanding and respect if we don't allow ourselves to delve into the painful topics and address the real issues of this conflict?

By now, you may be noticing this is not a conflict of equals. Both the Zionist Israeli paradigms and Palestinian paradigms will be discussed in more depth.

The birth of modern-day Zionism is not being disputed here. It is clearly understood that Zionism was created to unite the Jewish people globally. The main flaw of Zionism and the subsequent modern-day creation of Israel is that they inaccurately claim that for over 2,000 years the Jewish people alone have continually been persecuted at the hands of their oppressors. They completely ignore the fact that they shared the land with other people who were equally persecuted and have been on that land for just as long. The Jewish people have never lived in the Holy Land on their own, and the whole area has been invaded and occupied by many empires seeking expansion.

Zionism has such a strong hold on the minds of its followers that many are offended when other people claim that they, too, have been equally persecuted throughout history. The Zionist machine, since its formation, has been so focused on its followers' mindsets that it has blinded many from the truth and created fear amongst its people in many ways. Imagine the impact on people when they are constantly being reminded at every opportunity that they have been victims throughout history and, if not careful, will be persecuted again in the future.

The Land of Palestine

In the eyes of many, the regime has dehumanized the Palestinian man, woman, and child, just as the Nazis dehumanized Jewish Europeans. This perpetual victimhood across the globe is killing us all slowly. It is turning brothers, sisters, cousins, friends, and neighbors against each other.

The Land of Palestine was never a land without a people. The name "Palestine" first appeared in the fifth century BCE when the ancient Greek historian Herodotus wrote of a "District of Syria," called Palestine, between Phoenicia and Egypt. Throughout the ages, it was a buzzing commercial trade center with great literature, theology, agriculture, and merchants. Palestine was a place where Muslim, Christian, and Jewish Palestinians lived together with respect and understanding.

There were situations where they all fought side by side protecting each other. Contrary to popular belief, historically, there has been respect for all faiths in this land. When Islam came to Palestine in the seventh century, Umar ibn al-Khattāb mandated that mosques only be built in a way that did not intrude on other faiths. That is why to this day, you see Churches on one side and Mosques on the other in any given area historically known as "Palestine." Islam itself recognizes both Jews and Christians as being people of the book and they do not require conversion as believers who have already surrendered to God. "Aslem" in Arabic means "surrender," and if you have already "surrendered" to God then Islam requires nothing more of any person. I'm only writing this section to help people understand what the term means. Duraid Lahham, a Syrian actor, activist, all-time great human being, and one of my childhood heroes explained it eloquently. He explained that "Kulna Aslamna" (we have all surrendered) applies regardless of whether you are Jewish, Christian, or Muslim (this includes all the factions and denominations). Even with Eastern spiritualism or new age spiritualism, the concept of surrendering is at the forefront of their teachings.

Judaism, Christianity, and Islam are part of Palestinian culture and heritage. Judaism came first, followed by Christianity, and then some 500 years later, Islam was introduced. Christian Palestinians are descendants of the first Christians in the world. Christianity began as a movement within Judaism at a time when the Jewish people had been dominated, culturally and politically, by foreign powers in Palestine. We cannot be certain of what proportion of people in Palestine converted from Judaism to Christianity and then to Islam, but we do know that these people have shared the same land since civilization began.

A Land of Cousins

The connection between the people of this land is undeniable, as DNA testing could easily demonstrate. There has never been a point in time when the Jewish people resided separately on any land, let alone in historic Palestine. They have always shared their common ground with their cousins, dealing with invaders and oppression together.

Why do I call them cousins? Because Judaism, Christianity, and Islam stem back to Abraham, who is traditionally considered to be the first Jew to have made a covenant with God. All three religions recognize Abraham as their first prophet and are known as the Abrahamic religions. Jews see themselves as the descendants of Abraham through his son Isaac, and his grandson, Jacob. Jacob was known as the father of the twelve tribes of Israel. Ishmael was the first son of Abraham, the collective patriarch of the Abrahamic religions, and he is considered to be a prophet in Islam and is followed by Christians.

The last time I was in Jerusalem was on the final day of the Jewish weeklong festival of Sukkot, which celebrates the gathering of the harvest. and commemorates the protection of God. During this time, one of the things that is prayed for is rain.

As I was walking out of the old city gates, I saw a couple of older Palestinian men look up to the sky as a light rain began to fall. One of the men looked at his friend and said, "Wallah Rabna biheb wilad ilaam," which translates to, "I swear to God, our Lord loves our cousins." The term "Wilad ilaam," means "cousins from the father's side of the family." That year was particularly dry, and the rains came on the last day of Sukkot. They both smiled and nodded in agreement as they went on their way.

This five-second interaction might seem of little value, but it stopped me in my tracks. I have never been able to let this memory go. At the time, I smiled as well, though maybe for a different reason. This comment ran so deep that from then on, I began to see things differently.

A few days after this incident, we were back in Haifa and decided to take the bus and spend the day on Carmel Beach. On the bus trip there, I noticed that next to me in the same row were a Jewish lady and a Muslim lady. In this instance, the only way to identify who was who was by the necklaces we wore. I had the Cross on, while the second lady was wearing the Star of David, and the third, the Crescent Moon. For me, it was a moment to realize how we have been taught to separate ourselves from one another, and then work on trying to find where we belong.

The act of wearing these necklaces may not seem significant at all, and there is beauty in it. Except, for me at the time, with my heightened sense of awareness when it came to the division we have created, it was yet another significant moment. I love the symbol of the Cross, as I am sure the other two ladies love the symbolic meaning of their own necklaces. However, as a result of that experience, I eventually took off my necklace and decided not to wear it again. Not because my faith had been weakened, but rather, because I no longer wanted to be identified and separated from my *wilad ilaam*, "my cousins."

These two small, yet profound moments in Jerusalem and on the bus in Haifa, helped me question it all. This whole mess that has been created in the Holy Land—all the suffering, oppression, activities that violate international laws, occupation, checkpoints and walls dividing communities, laws working against all traditional non-Jewish Palestinians—all for what? Deep down inside, if you are indigenous to the land and your faith, you will know that we are all brothers, sisters, and cousins. If you followed your faith from the heart, you would know we all come from the same source. The elements of division do not have to be this way; the only thing driving the current predicament is fear and separation.

Repeating the Cycle

There is fear on the Zionist side that if they do not protect themselves with everything they have, they will be persecuted as in the past. Therefore, there has to be a place where they can reside by themselves, surrounded by walls, checkpoints, a massive military army, and control. All this needs to be done with support from the West to protect them. Those joining the Israeli Defence Force (IDF) are taught to see every single Palestinian as their enemy. Even children are targeted in the occupied territories routinely.

According to Khaled Quzmar, general director, Defence for Children International in Palestine,

> *"...since 1967, Israel has operated two separate legal systems in the same territory. In the occupied West Bank, Israeli settlers are subject to the civilian legal system whereas Palestinians live under military law. No Israeli child comes into contact with the military courts. Israel has the dubious distinction of being the only country in the world that automatically and systematically prosecutes children in military courts. Each year, between 500 and 700 Palestinian children are tried in these courts, which, in practice and by design, deny fundamental fair trial rights and due process protections. This dual system offers no semblance of justice. From the moment Palestinian children come into contact with Israeli soldiers, their very basic human rights are denied. The majority of Palestinian children report being blindfolded, strip-searched, and subjected to physical violence at the hands*

of Israeli forces. Most Palestinian children are not informed of the reason for their arrest, and over half are forced to sign documents in Hebrew, a language they cannot read or understand. The Israeli military court's conviction rate is higher than 99 percent."

When I look at this objectively, my heart goes out to the Jewish people globally, with empathy and deep compassion. That may sound crazy. Here I am discussing Palestinian children being treated so unjustly by the system, yet I am sympathizing with Jews. Why would I do that? It's because I can see how the past is being repeated and will continue to repeat itself until we collectively break the cycle.

There was an incident during the third Intifada (Uprising) in 2014, when a Western reporter in Bethlehem asked a Palestinian woman on the streets what her view was of the current situation. Her response, even after the brutality and suffering at the hands of the IDF and all the curfews that applied to Palestinians was, *"We have been invaded on many occasions throughout history and we outlived all of them. This invasion is no different. We have done it before; we will do it again."*

While Palestinians recognize Judaism as being part of the Holy Land, they do not see the "new immigrants and settlers" as having a right to the land. They question:

- How can a blue-eyed, blond-haired Californian American Jew, or a German Jew, for example, have the right to their land and property? Judaism is a religion to them, just like Islam and Christianity is a religion, not a race.
- How, after over 2,000 years, can people make a claim by force to their legally owned lands?
- How is the world allowing this land confiscation and brutality to happen?
- Why is Palestinian life not as worthy as any other life?

- Why is the non-Jewish Palestinian population treated with such callous disregard?
- Why are Palestinians paying the heavy price for the suffering of the Jewish people in Europe, and other areas in modern times, that had nothing to do with them?

The biggest concern for the Jewish people is that by focusing so much on what they fear and do not want, they are merely creating a stage for exactly what they do not want to keep playing out. It's the perfect recipe for disaster, and it is creating their future based on past events. The formation of Israel has divided Palestinians geographically, politically, and religiously in an attempt to weaken their position.

Strategic Fragmentation: Divide and Conquer

To some significant degree, it worked at a leadership level. Compared to Zionist leadership, Palestinian leadership is currently weaker. One could argue it has always had its weaknesses, as it has been far too fragmented and there has been an adoption of centralized leadership over the years. This has not served Palestine well. Historically, Palestine has never had an army of its own, and its leadership has been assigned through occupation and invasions. Since 1948, there has been a concerted effort to keep its people divided by strategically fragmenting Palestinian communities into different sectors divided by walls, and also not allowing refugees the right of return.

While there have been attempts to date, Palestinian leadership remains much weaker than its counterparts. It's the classic divide-and-conquer strategy that seems to have worked on some fronts but not on others. In its current state, Palestinian leadership cannot claim a strategy for national liberation, service delivery, or representation— three elements needed for strong leadership and future growth. Is there truly a clearly defined goal, as a collective, from Palestinian leadership? Or is the current Palestinian authority merely a puppet and extension of the Israeli regime?

Zionism has had a clearly defined goal since its inception. In 1897, Theodor Herzl convened the first Zionist Congress in Basel, Switzerland, which outlined the Basel program, stating that *"Zionism strives to create for the Jewish people a home in Palestine, secured by public law."* This goal has been pursued with unwavering dedication. Over time, the movement has united Jewish communities globally (from an outsider's perspective) and demonstrated strong representation in Western politics and media. Some believe this representation also extends into sectors such as banking and mining, as well as the creation of influential lobby groups in the West. However, it is important to recognize that these perceptions are sensitive among Jewish groups, who caution against the spread of stereotypes that could further perpetuate misconceptions or myths.

Funding Division

According to Reuters, on September 15, 2016 the United States signed a deal with the Israeli government to give them $38 billion in military assistance over a period of ten years. This was the largest military aid package in U.S. history. Israel's total military budget in 2022 alone was around $22.6 billion.[1] Now, let me put this in perspective for us all. It is estimated that there are approximately 15 million Jews and 14 million Palestinians recognized in the world.[2][3] Many Palestinians are not represented in this statistic, and we can assume the same for the Jews. For argument's sake, let's say there is a combined total of just over 30 million Jews and Palestinians in the world, out of a total of 8 billion people. Why, therefore, would you possibly need $26.4 billion in military spending per year to wreak havoc in the world, when instead you could create a safe space for all on the one land? Imagine how far the $26.4 billion a year would go toward building the right social and commercial infrastructure for all people.

Does it not seem like madness to you when put so simply? How much more money is spent on creating hate and division per year, which is getting us nowhere, instead of using that money to create something of value for all? Why would you choose fear, hate, and separation over growth, evolution, and harmony?

While Palestinian leadership at present is lacking, Palestinian people are very strong and resilient, despite their current predicament. For a short while, it did seem like the attempt to divide its people was successful. Those two-plus million living within the 1948 borders felt like they had been forgotten as they became officially known as "Arab Israelis." Those living in the West Bank and Gaza may have felt the remaining Palestinians of '48 had sold out, and that life was much easier for them than in Gaza, the Occupied Territories, or as a refugee in the Arab countries. Over time, and to some degree in comparison, life had become easier for Palestinians in the 1948 borders than for others. But it is all relative.

From the very beginning, all Palestinians have been denied their rights to return to their seized homes and belongings, lands, and self-identification. To even call yourself Palestinian or hold the Palestinian flag became an offense, and you had to refer to yourself as an Arab-Israeli. The school curriculum has also been controlled, and Palestinians have not been permitted to teach their history. Funding for schools differs greatly for Israeli Arabs in comparison to Israeli Jews.

Guilty by Association

The list goes on...when my uncle on my father's side was imprisoned and jailed for political reasons, the whole extended family was implicated by association. Another uncle was jailed, his daughter exiled after she fled the country, houses raided, and fear set in, since you never knew who would be watching, listening and what would happen next. My uncle, Dahoud Tourky, was one of the Palestinians living within the 1948 borders of what is now known as Israel proper, as an "Arab Israeli." He is one of the first Palestinians within the 1948 borders to have established a movement with Jewish comrades against the state of Israel. He was the leader of the united Jewish-

Arab left-wing group called the Red Front, which was an anti-Zionist group. My uncle served fourteen years in prison and was only released due to a prisoner exchange agreement between Israel and Syria.

It was not an easy time for my family, or any family living in these borders. Constant vigilance was required in terms of what we said, and to whom we said it. We were, and continue to be, treated like second-class citizens, at best.

When I was nine years old, we had just returned from England where my parents were studying at the University of Birmingham. There, we all experienced what it was like to be free and to have a voice. On return to Haifa, my older brother and I returned to our old school. One day, my mother received an urgent phone call from the headmistress, asking her to come down to the office at the school due to an incident. In many other countries, if a parent gets an urgent call to come into the headmaster's office, you can guess that your child has gotten into a fight or some other mischief. In this case, when my mother arrived at the school, the principal felt she needed to talk to her immediately. It turned out that my brother had been "caught" by one of the teachers drawing the Palestinian flag on his book in class, and this needed to be addressed quickly due to fear of repercussions.

Symbols of Resistance

Imagine, for one second, how drawing a flag on a schoolbook could create fear to the extent that it needed to be addressed immediately. As a child, I could not understand why what my brother had done was of such consequence, but it gives you an idea of the absurdity of life as a Palestinian in his or her own land.

Even today, we have to ask ourselves questions. Is this really how we want to live? Regardless of where you are in the world, do we think this is how we should be treating each other? Do you know how easy it is for those "Others" to become "Us"?

Do the Israelis live in such fear, that if a child were to draw a

Palestinian flag, there could be consequences for that child and his/her family? My brother and many others went on to draw many more flags over the years in defiance. At one stage, to avoid retribution in Gaza, West Bank, and in the borders of 1948, Palestinians adopted drawing the watermelon in public, as it represented the colors of the Palestinian flag. The cut watermelon became a symbol of resistance. This in itself gives you an idea of the Palestinian people's psyche, regardless of its leadership, as compared to the Jewish people's psyche in the Holy Land today.

When you study the history of the region where oppression prevailed, you learn that over time, those who are oppressed will resist. It happened in South Africa, India, the United States with slavery, as well as in Nazi Germany, and it will continue to happen. The Israeli regime is becoming desperate. The harder it tries, the more pain is inflicted, the more afraid its people become, and the more resistance they will experience.

With all that has happened over the years and with the advent of social media, regardless of the almighty algorithm, Palestinian identity has grown stronger and stronger. Since 1948, Israel, with all its funding, has attempted to weaken and even deny the Palestinian identity to build a new and strong cultural identity globally. In a world where people are now encouraged to identify themselves however they desire, be it she/he/non-binary, etc., imagine a people not being allowed to identify as their nationality or raise their flag because it has been made illegal. The Israeli government has attempted to rewrite history by trying to erase Palestinian history, but all it is doing is strengthening the Palestinian identity worldwide. All the land confiscation, cultural misappropriation, illegal home demolition, separation and apartheid laws, and even severe restrictions have not weakened the Palestinian identity. All their actions and attempts are driving a stronger Palestinian identity and generating greater unity in all of the geographically divided sectors.

Social media has become the Palestinian people's tool to bring people together. They resist the imposed separation through the denial of a refugee's right of return, through all the checkpoints and walls they have put up. Mainstream media may be unwilling to tell you what is going on in this area, but social media is its nemesis. No matter how poor or underprivileged you are, no matter how oppressed you are, the vast majority of people these days have a phone and access to Wi-Fi. There is no more hiding; fortunately, transparency is becoming the norm.

Despite Israeli government-funded programs that spin stories on social media and pay thousands of people to troll posts they see as "the Palestinian online social media threat," the online guerrilla warfare continues unabated. It is not directed by any one group. This online social media presence is coming from every angle, by regular people all over the world. You cannot combat that or control it.

For an oppressor, the most "dangerous" people to watch out for are those who have nothing more to lose. In this instance, Palestinians have reached that point. Globally, we are at a critical moment in history, and the more brutal a regime becomes (as we saw with Nazi Germany and with South African Apartheid), the clearer we can see the end is coming.

It was evident only recently after Shireen Abu Akleh, a prominent Palestinian journalist whose assassination by the Israeli military was caught on a phone camera and shared globally. At the time, Shireen was reporting for Al Jazeera on the Israeli activities in the area of Jenin, which had escalated considerably. Her assassination prompted worldwide discontent among Palestinians, and even though Western media and news attempted to whitewash the incident, you could see the desperation and lengths the Israeli army and government were willing to go to to oppress the Palestinian people.

At Shireen's funeral, fully armed Israeli soldiers were sent to break groups of people up. Those carrying her coffin were beaten with batons as they refused to allow the coffin to drop to the ground. Muslim Palestinians were refused entry into the church and funeral, as Shereen was a Palestinian Christian, yet Palestinians are renowned for praying together at such events. Palestinian Christian priests and Muslim sheikhs will often pray together and lead their people as a united front. The Al Aqsa Mosque is a symbol of Palestine and is in the heart of all Palestinians regardless of their religion. Personally, I will pray at the Al Aqsa Mosque with all my brothers and sisters.

Can you imagine what it would be like if we could have rabbis, priests, and sheikhs pray together and lead all their people collectively in the Holy Land?

Watching the images on TV and on social media of fully armed Israeli soldiers beating the coffin carriers at Shereen's funeral brought back the images of the fifth and seventh stations of the cross where Christ was being whipped by Roman soldiers on their horses as he carried the cross. Upon falling, Simon of Cyrene came and took his place to relieve him. That is exactly what was happening at Shereen's funeral. The crowd would not allow her casket to fall that day in Jerusalem as Israeli soldiers were beating unarmed, mourning Palestinian pallbearers. As soon as a mourner was about to collapse from the beatings, another would step in to take his place.

This scene struck a chord. Jesus of Nazareth was born to Jewish parents in Palestine and started a global revolution. Palestine is where Christianity was born and where Jesus was crucified in Jerusalem over 2,000 years ago. He experienced the same torment as what was happening that day in 2022 at a modern-day funeral. The oppressor's name has changed, but history has an amazing way of repeating itself because we are still focusing on and creating the same thing over and over again. We are creating everything that we fear due to separateness.

How can we possibly dehumanize any individual, or collective like this? How can one human lose all sense of compassion for another human and become so desensitized?

Fear is at the heart of it all. And fear will be the downfall of powers that be as they take these extreme measures to "defend" their position.

At this point, some people may be saying this is a one-sided argument. What about terrorism? What about the rockets from Gaza? What about Hamas?

I want to make it clear. A Jewish life is equal to a Palestinian life, and vice-versa. The goal here is to help people realize that we must first be honest about what is going on, which will enable us all to seek justice and peace on equal terms.

Just before the pandemic hit us globally in 2020, I had been invited to present at a synagogue in Sydney with a Palestinian friend of mine, Issa, a refugee from Jordan. We were part of a small group of Palestinians and Jews in the Partners for Peace group. Around seventy Jewish people were attending the synagogue that day, led by a rabbi originally from California. I presented my section and explained my background and dream, as did Issa. Some of the audience were feeling quite uncomfortable and visibly upset by a few of the comments we were making concerning our rights in the Holy Land and our personal family stories. A few questions were directed at us, such as, "Why can't you all just go to another Arab country and leave us alone? Israel is the only Jewish country, whereas there are many Arab countries you can all go to." Another comment came up around the refugee status of Palestinians, "Why could they not just become citizens elsewhere?" as if they all wanted to remain refugees on purpose. We were also asked a question about the "hostility towards Jews in Israel back in 1948, and why did the Palestinians fight back at the time?"

It became really clear how fear can change the perception and beliefs of people and close them off from seeing different views and opinions. The rabbi and our Jewish friends on that day were of great support. It was the rabbi who jumped in on the last comment and spoke to his constituent, "You have to remember that it was us that came back to the land and other people were living on that land. They were defending themselves."

This is the ultimate truth. After the Holocaust in Germany, many European Jews came to Palestine seeking refuge. Palestinians did open their homes and hearts to help wherever possible. It was only when it was realized what was about to happen that Palestinians took exception. This day at the synagogue in Sydney was one of the first times I had heard that point of view being acknowledged so openly in a situation like this, by a Jewish rabbi. It gave me hope.

When addressing the question of why Palestinians could not just go and live in another Arab country, I explained that that was like asking someone from Thailand why they can't go and live in Korea, because they're all Asian countries, right? Or asking an American to leave everything behind, pack up a small number of belongings and go live in Canada because they're all North American and speak English.

One of the audience members admitted after the event that she had never seen it in that light. She had never considered it from the point of view presented, which surprised me because it seemed so obvious. There was a real example of how perception, our belief system, repetition of the same message, and fear work hand in hand to separate us from one another. If you repeat something often enough, people will start to believe it to be true if it is not questioned. A single belief is nothing more than a thought that has been repeated enough times, never questioned, and then accepted to be true at a subconscious level. Remember that we have 400 billion bits of information coming at us in any one second, and we are only aware of 2,000 bits of this information. Therefore, how can we not allow ourselves to at least entertain new ideas before accepting a thought as truth in all situations? It doesn't matter what the subject is—be it about the Jewish people, the Palestinian people, your relationships, work, social life, or even the thoughts you have about yourself.

As mentioned previously, by the time we are thirty-five years old, 50% of what we talk about regarding our past is not true, or is made up. Therefore, we are drawing upon faulty data to make our decisions. At what point are we going to question the current "truth" that we choose to believe if we are basing our views on past corrupted data?

You can change a belief if the assumption preceding it changes. I often ask myself questions when I feel out of sorts for any reason, like, "What am I not seeing? What assumption have I made to believe this? How can I see this differently? Do I want to believe this? Who can help me see this differently if I am feeling stuck? When we look deeply at, and explore the origins of, our beliefs and are willing to at least entertain new possibilities, we empower and give ourselves a chance to lead and make a difference in this world.

We have to be able to ask ourselves, "What is the truth anyway?" Yesterday's truth is not today's truth. If you set sail to as far as the eye can see, you are not going to drop off the end of the earth. That is our new truth, yet people adamantly believed that to be true at one time, and it was forbidden to question it, until it was proven otherwise.

"Absence of evidence is not evidence of absence."

— *Edzard Ernst*

I have heard so many people say, "It's impossible to solve this problem between the Jews and Palestinians." I, and hopefully now you, refuse to accept that belief which is based on a flawed assumption. When someone says the word *impossible*, the first question that comes to mind is, what truth is this based on? The imagined truth? The apparent truth? Or the ultimate truth?[4] What data set was used to make that assumption? Corrupt data, or data based on what we want from an open heart and what we want to create for our future?

If you can see it on the screen of your mind, you can create it in your reality. Nothing has ever been created without it being seen on the screen of someone's mind first. There are many today who clearly see it on the screen of their minds, including myself, and feel in their hearts that there is a way forward, and collectively we can create the ultimate truth.

We will do this one person at a time until we have the critical mass needed to change. It will create momentum and feel like "peace on equal terms" came quickly. We have evidence of this with the end of the South African apartheid regime in the early 1990s (formed in 1948), as well as the fall of the Berlin Wall in 1989. We will soon be celebrating the return of all refugees, the bringing down of more walls, and the celebration of peace in the Holy Land. People everywhere will be astounded by the speed at which it has happened. That is the beauty of momentum, which in and of itself is nothing more than mass in motion.

When presenting at the synagogue that day, I also made a point to the audience, "If you spend two weeks with me and get to know me, you will fall in love with me, and when you do that, you will fall in love with my people." I did not say that from a place of ego or arrogance. I said it because as human beings, we are wired to accept each other, and we are all connected as soon as we open our hearts. It's inevitable.

Mother Teresa was quoted as saying, *"If I look at the mass, I will never act. If I look at the one, I will."* There is a psychological phenomenon called psychic numbing that causes us to feel indifferent to the suffering of large numbers of people. Mother Teresa knew this only too well. This phenomenon is an interesting study of human behavior. As humans, we are emotionally driven creatures who can suffer from "compassion fatigue" and do not operate on logic when it comes to making decisions. We can numb ourselves and brush off mass tragedy. Yet, when one person needs help and is suffering, we can act quickly to engage to ensure their well-being and survival. We are so emotionally charged, and the media knows exactly how to play on this. No one is immune to this, as we can all be manipulated and fall into this trap if we are not consciously aware of it. Once you become aware of it, you can change the way you think and your perspective to "love your enemy." You are then able to show true compassion for all human beings, regardless of what side they sit on and who is "right or wrong."

It takes practice, and it does start by getting to know the "other" intimately and with genuine effort. Once you spend time getting to know your perceived "enemy" as a human being, you'll likely choose to live day to day with them on an equal basis; you will quickly learn how much we all have in common. You will surprise yourself and begin to understand life through their eyes. Your heart will open to them and your whole perspective will change. This is incredibly powerful. So, when we spend two weeks together getting to know each other with genuine care and on an equal footing, we learn to love the other person, and subsequently their people, because their people become your people. There is no separateness, there is only oneness, once you break down the physical and emotional walls allowing everyone to flourish with equality and equity.

While it may seem like an impossible task, many from both sides know and believe we can do better than what we are doing today. One such person is Noam Shuster-Eliassi, who is a freelance comedian, performer, peacebuilder, and activist. Noam is a graduate of Brandeis University, in Massachusetts, and grew up in Neve Shalom Wahat Al Salam ("Oasis of Peace"), situated between Jerusalem and Tel Aviv-Jaffa, which is the only community where Jews and Palestinians live together by choice, on equal terms.

"The community was established in 1970 by Fr. Bruno Hussar on the land of the Latrun Monastery. It is a model of equality, mutual respect, and partnership that challenges existing patterns of racism and discrimination as well as continued conflict. The community has established educational institutions based on its ideals and conducts activities focused on social and political change. Many of the village members work on peace, justice, and reconciliation projects. It has a population of more than 70 families and will grow to 150 families."[5]

Noam's parents moved to this community when she was young, and she grew up living with Palestinians on equal terms. Her work aims to bring justice and peace to Palestinians as she believes the existence of "Israel" cannot survive without Palestinians, and other identities cannot be wiped out whilst Israel builds a new one. Noam's father is an Ashkenazi Jew (Central or Eastern European Jew) whose parents were Holocaust survivors from Romania, while her mother is a Mizrahi Jew (Middle Eastern or North African Jew) from Iran. She learnt quickly that the Israeli Independence Day celebration was a day her neighbors and friends mourned as it was the day of catastrophe for them. Noam shares with *Brandeis Magazine* (Spring/Summer 2019), "The narrative of the Holocaust we grew up on is that something terrible happened to us—which it did—and we do not have the space or place to talk about other suffering. We don't train that muscle to talk about pain collectively, or as something that happened in other places. This is preventing us from seeing Palestinian pain..."

It is intriguing to observe from the outside how we collectively have blinded ourselves from seeing the pain of the Palestinian people. When it comes to watching the suffering of another on the news, we have desensitized ourselves, and this phenomenon of "psychic numbing" has never been more obvious since the recent attention Western media has had on the events in Ukraine. What an eye-opener that has been. If you asked people randomly on the street if they believe one human life is equal to another, they would most likely respond by saying, "Yes, all human life is equal." Yet, when we face certain events, it seems that this response comes with a caveat. The answer becomes more like, "Well, you know, it depends," or, "It's a little more complicated than that, isn't it?"

There is nothing complicated about this. It is really simple. We either value all life equally, or we do not. When pictures were taken of the average Ukrainian making Molotov cocktails, it was hailed by the media as heroic, and they applauded the Ukrainian people's resistance and strength in defending themselves. Yet, when Palestinians are shown to do the same thing, it is labeled as an act of terrorism. There was a photo of a young girl standing up to a fully armed and equipped soldier, and the world hailed her as a hero when it was posted as a Ukrainian girl standing up against a Russian soldier. Yet, when it was revealed that this photo was taken some years back and in fact, it was an eleven-year-old Palestinian girl (Ahed Tamimi) from the Palestinian-occupied territories, the world went silent. When footage of the bombing of buildings was posted as Russian attacks on

Ukrainian civilians, the world cried out in total objection. When it was revealed that this was an event that had recently taken place in Gaza, and it was actually the Israeli Army attacking Palestinian residential buildings, the world went quiet again. Can you see how easily we can be played as humans? It is something each of us needs to become aware of. We all have our own biases, we can all be manipulated, and each one of us has our view of the world largely depending on how we were raised.

Noam Shuster-Eliassi, as an example, shows us that when we are willing to open up and remove fear from our hearts, sit with the other and listen to understand rather than to respond, we will find our common ground; we will see the ultimate truth and we will each want to work towards peace and justice for all.

The question always comes back to this: What do you want to create? What do we want to collectively create? Do we want to turn a blind eye and keep doing what we are doing? Nothing is impossible, and where there is one example, there are plenty of others. If it can be realized at an individual or community level, it can be realized on a state, country, regional, and global level.

∾

Chapter 12

THE CHANGE

A Shift in Perspective, Advocating Unity, Understanding, and Acceptance

"We cannot solve problems at the same level of thinking that we were at when we created those problems."
– Albert Einstein

L ife is all about choices. With every breath and action taken, we are constantly making decisions. Whether we realize this or not is another question. So, as we come to the end of the book, the real question is:

What will we do about this?

Do we want to keep focusing on what's not working in the world, and how challenging it is? Or do we want to focus on what is working, where the commonalities are, and bring ourselves back to our natural state of being? Will we accept that we are all connected and that we can make a difference?

Every single person can choose to play a part in making a real difference in this world. Do not underestimate your power. You can choose to be the source, rather than the seeker. To get started, we must allow ourselves to entertain new ideas and ask questions. The solution is much easier than we think, if we ask all the right questions.

Returning to the beginning, the solution can only come from ordinary individuals in Palestine, Israel, Europe, North and South America, Australia, and all across Asia. Individually, we hold the potential to effect change. The powers that be will listen when we create this mass consciousness. They will have no choice but to listen. We have seen examples throughout history of this, from Jesus Christ to Gandhi, from Martin Luther King to Nelson Mandela. We have seen great shifts and changes.

When we have the right solution based on equal terms, we will see that other problems around the world fix themselves and dissolve. There is a reason why as a race we have spent 92% of our time in conflict. It's because we have refused to understand why people do what they do. We do not spend enough time understanding ourselves, let alone others. This does not excuse inappropriate behavior, but once you start to gain understanding, your whole perspective changes. If the other person does the same, their whole perspective changes. All of a sudden, we find ourselves operating from the heart at a meaningful level, and we let go of fear, hatred, and the need to be right. We collectively let go.

There was an attempt to assassinate Pope John Paul II in 1981. He was shot four times before his would-be assassin was apprehended and eventually sentenced to life in prison. Pope John Paul II, in seeking to understand, asked his assassin why he did what he did. The assassin and the Pope became pen pals, and over time, he was forgiven publicly. He was eventually granted a full pardon and set free upon the Pope's request.

Is there a place for understanding unacceptable behaviors in the world? Forgiveness is not to be confused with pardoning, condoning, excusing, forgetting, or denying. Understanding aids forgiveness and then calls for moderation. We have to ask ourselves where the common ground is.

I was recently asked, "Well, what is the solution to such a complex situation? How are we going to bring peace to the region, given that all attempts have failed to date? Is the only possible solution a two-state solution? And what does peace look like?"

I can't repeat this often enough: it's not complicated. It will take a lot of work, and it may be hard as we have created so many problems within the sectors that we are aware of, and many that we don't even know exist yet, but it is fixable. Everything is fixable, especially when people are ready for it. When people are ready to listen, be heard, and open to true dialogue, the answer will come.

Previous attempts have not been true attempts, based on equal terms for both parties. To date, there have been veiled attempts to benefit one over the other. Even the Oslo Accord in 1993 was skewed to disadvantage the Palestinian population, and the Israeli government never had any intention of letting go of illegal settlements. We have to ask ourselves the question of why a two-state solution may not work as well. Could it be because it is not the natural state of being? We should also ask, "When in the history of mankind has the land been occupied by only one people?" The aim is not to definitely say it should be a two-state or a one-state solution. My personal belief is that even if it starts as a two-state solution, it will eventually end in one. But again, that is just a personal point of view and I recognize there could be other ways of looking at this.

> From the River to the Sea, <u>All</u> People Will Be Free,
> *is the only solution. This is the ultimate truth:*
> Unless we are all free, no one is free.

A few things have to happen on both sides, of course, for us to finally see a just and peaceful resolution based on equal terms.

First, and most importantly, we have to accept that what has happened has happened, and there is nothing we can do to change the past. We need to learn from the past to help us move forward. We need to be willing to accept that *never again* means *never again for all people*. It cannot be selective. One human life equals another human life, regardless of religious or ethnic orientation.

Second, we need to acknowledge the events of the past and not attempt to hide or wipe out history and wrongdoings. Just as the German government apologized to the Jewish people, the Israeli government will need to, at the very minimum, acknowledge the events that have taken place against the non-Jewish Palestinians since 1948. Acknowledgment is the first step to healing. The denial of events from 1948 onwards is painful to Palestinians, as Israel and much of the world deny the catastrophe that took place, and continues to happen.

And finally, there needs to be an agreement that no matter what, all people will be granted the same rights, at every level. If people want there to be a country with true "democracy" in the Middle East, then you have to afford every resident the same rights. To have a state running an apartheid regime claiming it's the only democracy in the Middle East while the world superpowers watch on in support, is the definition of an oxymoron. For example, the right of return has to be afforded on the same terms for Palestinians as it currently applies to Jews.

This is where things get interesting and people struggle the most. "Well, what would you call the country? How is everyone going to agree? The other people will just want to kick us out eventually, won't they? There will no longer be an Israel over time. Or will there ever be a state of Palestine again?" The questions go on and on, suggesting the extreme difficulty of it all, because we are focusing on what we already know rather than what we actually want.

What if we were to look at this from a new perspective and build a new model? Where is the common ground?

For example, Palestinians of all religious backgrounds from any part of the country believe that the land is the "Holy Land." Jews all over the world, regardless of where they are, believe that the land is the "Holy Land." Everyone in the world refers to this area of land as the "Holy Land." This is the first major and most significant thing we all have in common.

This is hard to comprehend, even for myself as a Palestinian and all the sentiments associated with it. The way things are today, calling it the "Holy Land" downplays the real issues, and many Palestinians believe it is a form of white-washing. But it has come to a point where we need to sit down and question everything. If we truly believe it is the Holy Land, how holy are we being when we deny the existence and rights of another?

If we believe that the blood of the land runs through our DNA, do you think the land cares what we call her? We belong to her; she does not belong to us.

> "Remember You are Dust and to Dust, You Shall Return."
>
> — *Genesis 3:19*

We came from her, and we will go back to her, just like the wave to the ocean. Does the name matter? If so, could we call her the "Holy Land," then? I do not have all the solutions and don't claim adopting this name is the solution either, but these are some real concepts we should ponder and challenge ourselves with. This is merely a starting point to help us challenge our current thinking to help us create a new model.

The second major similarity is that we all acknowledge that Jews, Christians, and Muslims are people of the book and we come from the Abrahamic tribes sharing the same ultimate father. We all claim there is only one God. How are we not remembering this every day with every action we take? We all come from the same source, we will all go back to the same source, so why all the fuss? If you are a true believer, and not a follower of social media, news, and the distorted truth, you will then know this from the bottom of your heart.

A person cannot, on one hand, claim righteousness through their religion and on the other hand not follow the true word of God. We cannot allow ourselves to pick and choose. If any of us are going to claim the land, the second we attempt to divide and subjugate another and deny their rights, then we have no claim to her at all. This is regardless of whether you have been persecuted, or have become, or are about to become, the persecutor.

Another similarity is our Semitic roots. We are all Semitic and the whole notion of antisemitism in Palestine/Israel and where it is being taken today is nothing short of absurd. Just because people do not agree with the current state of affairs does not make them anti-semitic or even anti-Jewish. Antisemitism in Europe and the United States has nothing to do with the Palestinian people, yet every day they pay a price.

All those who are from the Holy Land share the same Semitic heritage. And though Hebrew and Arabic differ as languages, there are many similarities as well. What we do share is that we have all been oppressed and continue to be oppressed in one way or another. If we stop and take the time to ruminate on the situation, we will realize how much we have in common, including our pain. Why not use that for good rather than create further suffering?

And a final point of similarity: we are all living, breathing human beings. We all share the same wants, needs, and dreams. How much more similarity do we need to keep looking for? There are groups in Israel/Palestine, like the Parents Circle-Families Forum (PCFF), and a joint Israeli-Palestinian organization, that are dedicated to reconciling communities through education to achieve peace. This group is now made up of more than 600 families who have lost a loved one in the conflict. They share real pain and, while others may claim that one side has suffered more than the other, these families understand that pain is pain. Why not use this pain to ensure a much brighter future for the sake of our children, and for their children down the line? Why not dream of a much better future? Why not dream beyond borders?

Martin Luther King Jr, when delivering his iconic speech in August 1963, did not once say, "I have a strategy," or, "I have a plan." He said, "I have a dream." He imagined a future in which "the sons of former slaves and the sons of former slave owners" could "sit down together at the table of brotherhood;" a future in which his four children are judged not "by the color of their skin but by the content of their character."

There is still a lot of work to do in this area in the United States of America, but the point of his speech was that he was able to put the past behind him, learn from it, and forge a way forward to end the division, and then commence to unite people on equal terms. It all has to start with a dream, and if enough of us hold on to that dream, we can take daily action to fulfill it until momentum takes full effect.

First, we have to be willing to let go of what we think we know and believe in order to create a new belief system. We need to embrace our similarities and change that one central notion of separatism that we have created. We all share the same God, and we are not separated from God. If we are going to use religion, let's use it for unification rather than separation. Start understanding the other person from their point of view.

> *"You can't understand another person's experience until you've walked a mile in their shoes."*
>
> — Mary T. Lathrap, *Judge Softly,* 1895

Just the act of sitting down and getting to know the other person on equal footing will have a significant impact.

When people claim a one-state solution will never work, reject that notion, and ask these questions instead:

- Why could it not work?
- What do I choose to believe?
- What if it could work?
- How did it work in the past when Jews, Christians, and Muslims lived together in Palestine?
- What examples do we have to support the idea that this can work?

- How was apartheid in South Africa dismantled?
- What needs to happen for it to work?

Nelson Mandela stated in 1997: *"The United Nations took a strong stand against apartheid; and over the years, an international consensus was built, which helped to bring an end to this iniquitous system...we know too well that our freedom is incomplete without the freedom of the Palestinians."*

He saw the similarities of South Africa's apartheid state to that of the current Israeli state. He also acknowledged publicly that: *"All of us need to do more in supporting the struggle of the people of Palestine for self-determination."*

The last question above is one of my favorite questions because for this great dream to finally be realized, several things need to happen. Collectively, we must realize that while there is always an end to everything, the way we are going about it will not solve the problem, no matter what the goal is.

There was a Zionist dream of a single homeland in Palestine for Jews with no regard for the non-Jewish Palestinians who had resided on the land throughout the ages. This was never going to work and was always going to backfire at some point in time. Like every other regime that is based on oppression, this, too, will end at some point. The question again is, how do we want it to end? Do we want to keep repeating the cycle or do we want to finally end it on our collectively beneficial terms? It is that simple, and it is all about choice.

For Palestinians, with the newly created State of Israel, there needs to be a mindset shift as well. Regardless of what has happened in the past, they have to recognize that over the past seventy-four years, a new culture has been formed. Even if the person in Israel is a European Jew or Middle Eastern Jew from another country, they now live in the same land.

With seventy-five years of history, there are up to three generations of children who only know this land. What has been imposed on Palestinians cannot be done in return to these children. They cannot be thrown out, or treated in the same way Palestinians have been treated since 1948 when the current regime does eventually come to an end. We collectively have to be willing to end the cycle of oppression, and those currently oppressed must avoid becoming the oppressor at all costs, otherwise, we will start the cycle again. There has to be an acceptance that never again means never again for all.

As previously stated, in total, there are approximately 30 million people globally who identify as being Jewish or Palestinian. Even if every single person were to choose to live in the Holy Land (Palestine pre-1948 borders), there would be plenty of room for all.

The current state of Israel proudly boasts being the "start-up nation with innovation at its core." According to the jewishlibrary.org, in 1918 the Jewish population in Palestine was 8.1% of the total population. By 1947, it was at 32% as many Jewish refugees were taken in after the events of World War II, and the Holocaust. In 1948, as a result of the expulsion of Palestinians, that percentage grew to 82.1% (716,700 Jews vs. 156,000 non-Jewish Palestinians that remained in the '48 border). What Zionism did not factor into its plans was the Palestinian population growth within the 1948 borders.

As of September, 2022, the number of Jews in the 1948 borders is just over 7 million people, partially as a result of birth rates, but mostly government-supported migration. However, the Palestinian "Arab Israelis" number over 2.5 million, purely as a result of birth rates. The total number of Palestinians in the historical Palestine borders is approximately 7.2 million, with 670,000 illegal settlers living in the occupied territories.

The remainder of Palestinians (5.6 million) are either living as refugees, for many in appalling conditions in the Arab countries, or reside as citizens/residents/refugees around the world. Approximately, 6.8 million Jews are living outside of Israel by choice.

The point of this recap is to illustrate that if the Israeli government can so meticulously plan for this population growth of Jewish people from all over the world over a short time, we can plan, collectively, to accommodate all people from both sides. Not everyone is going to want to live in the Holy Land, so this figure is grossly exaggerated, but you get the point.

There is Enough for All

If we take all the money currently being poured into destruction and separation and utilize it instead for growth and prosperity, can you imagine what could be built? There is no shortage of money to realize this dream.

From the Palestinian side, with so many engineers, town planners, doctors, nurses, and teachers, there is certainly no shortage of expertise. Palestinians in general put a huge emphasis on education. Their priority is centered around supporting their children through higher education, despite their financial and political circumstances. Palestinians feel that while everything has been taken away from them, the one thing that can never be taken away is knowledge and education. They will go to great lengths to enter university and finish their degrees, and the number of Ph.D.-level qualified Palestinians by ratio, is one of the highest in the world, for both genders.

To be accepted into higher institutions in Israel, Europe, or other countries, including in the Arab world, and to gain sponsorship where needed, Palestinians know they have to work harder than anyone else. Like their Jewish cousins of the past, they know they need to work harder and smarter as a matter of survival.

Napoleon Hill stresses the benefits of accumulating specialized knowledge in his book *Think and Grow Rich*,[1] and what Palestinians are doing today is focusing on building that specialized knowledge where it will be needed worldwide. As an example, in 2016, it was reported in Israel21c.org that the Palestinian community of Arraba in the lower Galilee had more than six doctors per thousand inhabitants which was one of the highest numbers of doctors per capita in the world.[2]

Such Potential—If We Can Work Together

So, Israel is one of the world's leading innovative states, and Palestinians have one of the highest levels of education as a population. With all this specialized knowledge worldwide, there is no doubt that with the right goal and carefully staged planning, commercial and social infrastructure can be built to accommodate all on equal terms.

What is good for one person has to be good for the other. To bring a long-lasting and sustainable solution to the question of the Holy Land, no rules or laws can exist favoring one party over the other. Why can't pre-1948 borders be reinstated and all walls, checkpoints, fake borders, apartheid laws, and laws preventing Palestinians from the right to return be dismantled?

A Future for All

Let's look at what this means in practical terms:

The role of the international community to date has been very interesting to observe. Great Britain and the United States and a few other smaller players, including some Arab countries have played a supposed "mediation" role that has been destructive, rather than one of true commitment to justice and peace. The strong Zionist lobby groups in these countries have influenced their foreign policies and political agendas heavily.

In their current state, there is too much at stake and too much to lose, should they choose to support a just and equitable solution. Even those foreign parties and governments who support a two-state solution are doing so from fear of the strong Zionist lobby groups. They have not thought deeply enough about the ramifications of this, or they are simply using the statement as rhetoric with no real intention of bringing justice and peace to the land. The pressure must come from their constituents and from us, the people. When the pressure is strong enough, they will change.

We have many examples of civil disobedience across the globe which have led to significant change. There was Mohandas Gandhi's Salt March (India) in 1930, where Gandhi led a 240-mile march to the Arabian Sea to protest against the British salt monopoly, inspiring widespread civil disobedience. It eventually contributed to India's independence from British rule. There was also the now-infamous Rosa Parks bus boycott (USA). In 1955, where Rosa Parks refused to give up her seat for a white passenger on a bus in Montgomery, Alabama, leading to a 381-day bus boycott and the eventual desegregation of public transportation in the city. There was also the great Singing Revolution (Estonia, Latvia, Lithuania) between 1987 and 1991, where mass public singing events in these countries served as a form of peaceful protest against Soviet occupation. It ultimately led to their independence.[3]

Civil disobedience is simply a term used to describe active, non-violent refusal to accept the current terms of governments on specific matters. While we think that we have no say, we can make a difference, one person at a time, and together. There just has to be enough of us globally to influence change in the right way.

Giving up on creating the world we want to live in is not an option. Do a quick Google search to see where people made a difference through non-violent methods. From women's rights to reneging on segregation, from refusal to accept colonist taxes in India to the change to gay rights and same-sex marriage, from the end of South African apartheid to so much more. It can be done. We first must refuse the current players to act as mediators, and demand change in foreign policy in this area across the globe.

How *YOU* Are Either a Part of the Solution or a Part of the Problem

Study your current foreign policy and ask yourself how this is benefiting connection globally—or is it still about separation and oppression of the many for the benefit of the few? Currently, there is too much interference from the major world players, ensuring the situation in the Holy Land gets worse and worse. These current so-called "mediators" cannot play a part in the just and equitable solution unless they change their mindsets and agendas. Pressure needs to be placed on our governments to change their attitude on how they are supporting the apartheid regime for no reason other than violating human rights.

The funding that supports war and destruction must be stopped at the source. We, people from all sides, have to be ready to say, *"enough is enough!!"* It's your taxpayer money that is being used to fund wars and oppression. Is this what you want?

According to the United States Census Bureau, the official poverty rate in America in 2021 was 11.6%, with 37.9 million people living in poverty. Does this seem insane to you? We can use our funds to help our people domestically and even help other nations to bring peace to the region. Or we can use it to prolong death and destruction until, ultimately, we will all suffer even more from it.

When you vote, make your vote count by understanding your current representative's foreign policy in this matter. Send emails to all representatives and government bodies asking them about their stance on the Israeli/Palestinian matter. Ask them what their view on the current funding is. What is their solution, should they win the election, be it at a local level or national level? The emails you receive back or don't receive back will be very telling. Make your vote count. Because this matter will impact you and your loved ones, more than you can imagine, on many levels. So, send a clear message through your voting rights. You have the power.

There are also many groups in your area that can help you and are working towards a peaceful true solution.[4] Seek them out and use their resources to make it easier to understand. If you meet a group that seems to be one-sided and refuses to look at the picture with a true desire for peace with justice and liberation, walk away from them. They are not part of the critical mass that is being built.

'Hindering' Progress

There are two central issues at play, currently, that are hindering progress. The first is the issue of Jerusalem, which is being played out as we speak, in both the global arena, and domestically. The second is the question of the Palestinian refugees, and their right to return.

Again, we have to laugh at the absurdity of the current issues at play when it comes to the matter of Jerusalem and if it will be recognized as the capital of Israel, or Palestine. On December 6, 2017, President Trump formally recognized Jerusalem as the capital of Israel and stated that the American embassy would be moved from Tel Aviv to Jerusalem. Jerusalem has long been a point of contention and this act alone stirred up worldwide emotion.

The Morrison Government in Australia quickly followed to support this notion in an attempt to win local votes. The Liberal party lost the election in Australia and then the newly elected government in Australia quietly dropped this recognition, winding back their predecessor's language that had been adopted.

Furthermore, Liz Truss as the then-newly elected prime minister in Britain, declared that Britain did indeed recognize Jerusalem as the capital of Israel, and the British embassy would be moving from Tel Aviv, despite the fact that this move would violate British obligations under international law. This same prime minister tendered her resignation suddenly after only fifty days in office, as a result of public outcry on other matters.

Let us look at this more closely. When you visit Jerusalem, and as you walk through the old streets and gates, you quickly feel you are in God's presence, regardless of your political or religious affiliation. Jerusalem is one of the holiest of holy places in the world for the three oldest religions. The city of Jerusalem is a sacred place for all the Abrahamic religions and the one area shared between all three, is the Temple Mount.

Half the Baby

Any attempt to divide Jerusalem and recognize it as belonging to one but not the other is doomed to failure. This whole conversation itself now goes well beyond absurd and, in fact, could be the single most devastating move, globally. These political moves that have not been thought through will create a catastrophe that could impact us all, globally.

If you call yourself a believer in God, then you will know instinctively that Jerusalem cannot be divided. The act of division would destroy this holy place, and it could be the start of a conflict of a scale we have not seen before. Why would we even want to divide this place? It is a place for worship. "Palestinians will pray in the Churches as well as the Al Aqsa Mosque as Christians and Muslims. Jews pray at the wall and the Al Aqsa site is Holy to them." Why can't we continue to pray there together? Why create unnecessary unrest? Why enter the Al Aqsa, the holiest of sites, during the holiest of days in Ramadan and attack civilians during their deep prayers? Should we not be asking all these questions?

This reminds me of the biblical story involving King Solomon. The story is referred to as the *Judgement of Solomon,* where Solomon made a ruling between two women, both claiming to be the mother of a child. Solomon revealed their true relationship to the child by suggesting the baby be cut in two, with each woman receiving half. He was quickly able to determine the non-mother as the woman who approved of his proposal, while the real mother pleaded not to carry this act out and for the child to be given to her contender.

The same meaning from thousands of years ago still applies today. If you are a true believer, anywhere in the world, you will know that the answer is that this holy place is for all and cannot be divided. You cannot claim to be a true Christian, Muslim, or Jew and act in an unholy way. You do not belong to this place if you choose to follow division over unity. It is that simple. With a one-state solution if adopted, the question of Jerusalem will no longer be an issue, will it?

The Right to Return

The second contended issue is the question of the Palestinian refugees and their right to return. This issue goes hand-in-hand with the right to return of Jews globally, regardless of whether they are of Palestinian/Middle Eastern descent or European descent. If you start a conversation with people of strong opposing views, this topic itself can create wars.

Palestinians generally cannot understand how a European, American, or even Ethiopian Jew (or a person who has one Jewish grandparent) has the "right to return" to a country that was newly formed. In 1950, Israel passed a law and has since heavily funded this law, which gives Jews, people with one or more Jewish grandparents, and their spouses the right to relocate to Israel and acquire Israeli citizenship. The lost Jews (tribe) of Ethiopia were found under this law and brought to Israel on a fully funded scheme, providing them with free housing and other social support. Jews from the United States, for example, are also funded to "return" to Israel and settle on the illegally occupied territories of Palestine.

Palestinians question how this can be allowed, given that they are refused the right to return. How can you separate families from each other and not allow them to meet, or to return? For the most part, Palestinians believe the only Jews who have a right to live in the Holy Land are those who are Palestinian Jews. A German Jew belongs in Germany, and an American Jew belongs in America, etc. The consensus is that Judaism is a religion, just like Islam and Christianity, and other religions residing all over the world. It is not a nationality. Put simply, though, the time has come to accept and allow everyone the right of self-determination.

Palestinians crave the right to self-determination, and so this craving needs to be afforded to all Jewish people. If there are no more than 30 million people in total from both sides, and not all will want to reside in the Holy Land, this whole argument becomes irrelevant. What is right for one has to be afforded to the other, and after seventy-four years, Israeli Jewish identity has been formed, and we owe it to our children and their children to accept this.

On the other hand, if Jews, people with Jewish grandparents, and their spouses have a legal right to return, then we must afford the same rights to all Palestinians. There is no other way if we truly want to forge our way to peace and prosperity.

"Do unto others as you would have done unto you."

This golden rule needs to be applied in every situation given that we are all irrevocably connected. What you do to another, you do to yourself. This will help guide us towards calmness of mind, and speed of action.

Since the COVID-19 pandemic, it feels like globally, at an individual level as well as at a collective level, we are experiencing the opposite of this. We have no calmness of mind, and as a result, our actions are more harmful than beneficial. Let's just stop and ask ourselves the question before making any decision: "Is this how I would want to be treated?" If the answer is no, don't do it, and change your behavior. Yet again, it's simple when we start to reconnect and take the time to understand our true nature.

If we can relocate and integrate the lost tribes of Ethiopia and Jewish people from Texas so quickly, we can also relocate Palestinians back to their homeland just as effortlessly. We have enough town planners, engineers, and money to do so. For example, with over 70% of the people in Gaza also being refugees, we need to allow people to move freely and visit or live in any part of the country. The apartheid roads, gated pens, and heavily armed military personnel at checkpoints have to become a thing of the past. Could a one-state solution allow this when we build the right social and commercial infrastructure? According to Bob Proctor from the Proctor-Gallagher Institute, there are three things that people want the most.

1. They want to be free from financial concerns.
2. They want to enjoy how they spend their days.
3. They want to be surrounded by upbeat, positive enthusiastic people.

Stop for a few minutes here and think about what it is that you want. Make a written list of them. Do they all fit in one of the three points mentioned above? They will fit into one of those categories. So, why do we think it is different from anyone else? Separation makes us believe that somehow another person is different from us. They are not. Just because we have different traditions, food, culture, and may look different on the outside, this does not mean we are not all fundamentally the same, and that we aren't interconnected. It does mean that there is a richness of diversity we can all enjoy. We are all one sharing the same desires.

Build the right infrastructure to allow people to realize these three points, and you will quickly see how we can live the life we so desperately desire. When we allow everyone the same opportunities, we will change the dynamics, and allow everyone to flourish.

The issue of Palestinians' right to return is a critical one. If every Jew has the right to return, then every Palestinian must have the same right to return. If every Jew has the right to vote, then every Palestinian must have the right to vote. How can anyone argue that? Upfront, we have to acknowledge that some will want to leave the land if a one-state solution is adopted, as it will be difficult for them to adjust. If some cannot cope with this solution and decide to leave, then maybe, we should consider they are doing so because they did not really belong there in the first place or are not yet ready to call it home.

When building the social and commercial infrastructure, current laws need to be changed as well. Education funding needs to be revamped, and the walls of separation and checkpoints will need to be dismantled. Just like in South Africa, with the end of apartheid, there needs to be a step-by-step approach to building the new model. We can look at the steps taken there, learn from them, and even improve on them to pave the way forward.

Dismantling Apartheid

When apartheid was dismantled with democratic elections, countries across the globe lifted sanctions against South Africa to help create the newly formed government and state. The simple agreement is that no individual will be treated unjustly moving forward. All laws will apply to all people and not work in favor of one or the other.

This may even be easier than the dismantlement of the South African apartheid regime because the state of Israel is a newly created one, and the resources available to create brand new housing, roads, schools, hospitals, and so forth are in motion today. Much of this infrastructure did exist in Palestine already, but there has been a lot of work to support the influx of new immigrants into the country at a rapid rate.

Let's not forget this very important point; most of these projects and infrastructure rely heavily on Palestinian labor, which is currently being taken advantage of in both Israel proper and the occupied territories. Wages for Jews are generally higher than wages for Palestinians, and there are restrictions placed on travel to work for those Palestinians from the Occupied Territories and Gaza. Palestinians regularly require day passes to go through checkpoints designed to humiliate and dehumanize them. Palestinians can be waiting for hours in the heat in an overcrowded line, possibly fenced in. They are treated like cattle at best, while they watch their Jewish counterparts using a different route to either drive or walk past in comfort with no questions asked.

Israel heavily relies on the Palestinian (severely underpaid in many instances) labor force in all areas of its economy, so why not use it to build something of real value that will free all people once and for all? Such simple answers when you ask all the right questions.

~

Two weeks after signing my publishing deal, things escalated very quickly and five weeks on, we are watching the global and endless cries for a ceasefire. Hand-in-hand with that comes the release of the hostages. The ceasefire and the release of the hostages is but a first step. There is so much more needed, not just in action but in the head and heart of all. We are watching a minute-by-minute nightmare unfold in front of our eyes. If this does not move us, I am not sure what will. We need our media and the spin machine to be exposed and start changing the narrative. We as civilians must start to question everything. This has become a humanitarian catastrophe that has to stop and cannot be repeated—otherwise, if we are not careful, it will escalate globally. What is happening is painful to watch as the policy makers choose what to hear and not hear, ignoring the death toll and cries of innocent children and adults alike. There is a fundamental shift in thinking that is needed now, and we urgently need it to start.

We can call in the wisdom of our loving hearts to recognize the unity and commonalities and the universal rights of all to peacefully coexist with justice on equal terms. When we recognize and implement that, a glorious future becomes possible. There is no freedom for anyone until there is freedom for all. As hard as this is, and it does not matter which side you are on, we must all refuse to hate others, refuse the narratives we are being fed, choose our values carefully, and live by them regardless of the circumstances. For the sake of our shared humanity, be open to change. People fear a just peace as they may need to sacrifice some of their privileges. But in reality it is not a sacrifice, it is a step towards true freedom and prosperity. The alternative is so much better. I, for one, refuse to hate, and I refuse to give up on freedom for all on exact equal terms.

This is an issue that involves all of us and requires the active realignment of the citizens of the globe to come together. If you are sitting in a cafe enjoying a drink or conversation with a friend, if you are sure you will be able to return to your home safe tonight, if you care for your children and want the best for them, you are on the fortunate side of history for now. It is for all of us, not just those immediately affected by this, to stand up and take unequivocal responsibility for humanizing freedom now.

~

Practicing Love

Note From the Author

E very point, feeling, and idea presented here comes from a person who is neither a politician nor a historian. I just happen to be a woman, a human being who was born as a Christian Palestinian from Galilee. I have been fortunate enough to hold two passports, while the vast majority of Palestinians are longing for one. I can call myself a Palestinian and an Australian and know that I belong everywhere. I also hold a Canadian permanent residency and have been afforded the luxury (for many Palestinians it is still a luxury) of being able to travel and live in many different areas as an equal citizen with no legal prejudice or barriers.

Being a Palestinian gives me the advantage of having a triple dose of empathy for all human beings. My experiences and opportunities allow me to view different perspectives and understand intuitively what people have gone through and how they have suffered. I have spent many years honing this skill and continue to practice it with an open heart and with kindness at every opportunity.

It is uncomfortable when I know I have hardened my heart and closed it off. However, I am also aware that I still have a lot of work to do and need to keep practicing the art of love, and the concept of connectedness and oneness. It is a never-ending journey, and my hope is to help people and organizations begin to understand what is driving their behavior and the behavior of those around them.

I realize I don't have all of the answers, I simply believe there must be a better way. This "conflict" I mention does not need to be complicated. The same can be said about any other conflict we deal with in this world, be it on a personal or business/corporate level, or on the world stage. Self-leadership is the first step in all situations. To have great leadership at a global level, each one of us must first be a great self-leader. Take time to study yourself because the better you understand yourself, the better you will understand everyone else. We spend far too much time looking at other people in judgment, as a result of fear, and don't look at ourselves to see how we can be the solution to everything.

All of the answers lie with us as individuals, and then collectively, we can build whatever it is that we want, one step at a time. It is possible. We just have to believe that it is.

Start with yourself today. Work on developing your awareness and don't be afraid to ask questions to help you see different perspectives. We can then begin to work on a real solution for the Holy Land for all Palestinians and Jews on equal terms. When we have the solution and build this dream, you will be amazed at the number of other issues in the world that will dissolve right in front of our eyes...because it is all connected.

Don't allow yourself to be taken in by what you see on the news alone. Question it all and get to know the other to understand them better. Reject any idea that we cannot have a just and peaceful solution, and let's all be willing to do the hard work needed to get there. Everything we so desire and want is on the other side of fear. So, is it not worth it to understand our fears and act toward that goal, rather than allow fear to paralyze us and create more havoc?

The time has come for each of us to take a stance with an open heart and to say, "enough is enough!" Let's begin to build this dream today. Let's make sure we teach our children this concept of unity, love, and oneness from an early age. Only then will we be able to change things for ourselves and generations to come.

Together we can end the division. Together we can dream beyond borders.

~

In the cradle of ancient tales and whispered winds,
Where Palestine's essence in every heartbeat begins,
Lies a land steeped in poetry, music, and dance,
A symphony of love, a harmonious romance.
Amid olive groves and hills adorned with grace,
Resides a people whose spirit no borders can trace.
Their story, a mosaic of resilience and pride,
In the face of adversity, they stand side by side.
They seek not conflict, not wars or disdain,
But cherish the earth where their roots remain.
With humble staples, olive oil, za'atar, and more,
They celebrate life, a resilient folklore.
Their aspirations bloom in nurturing the young,
Education, laughter, songs softly sung.
Families gathering, in unity, to share,
The richness of culture, the love that's rare.
Generosity flows like a river's stream,
They give all they have, it's a heartfelt theme.
Their dignity, a beacon in times of despair,
Their pride, a testament, beyond compare.
Under the sun's gaze, on beaches they delight,
Hospitality shines, a guiding light.
For love and celebrations, their hearts take flight,
Embracing life with all their might.
They dream of the day when visitors may see,

The warmth of their welcome, the love set free.
Their strength unwavering, their spirits aglow,
In the path to return, their hopes ever grow.
Palestine, a haven of love, faith, and lore,
A land that yearns to open its door.
To share in their joy, their story untold,
Where love, not conflict, its treasures unfold.
They long for the day when full glory's embrace,
Shall greet them again in their sacred space.
Until then, they hold dear the love in their hearts,
For a time when peace weaves its harmonious parts.

Acknowledgement

I would like to extend my heartfelt gratitude to all those who have been instrumental in helping to bring *From the River to the Sea* to life. This book has been a journey of passion, introspection, and a deep commitment to fostering peace and justice for Palestinians and Israelis on equal terms. By resolving internal conflicts through an introspective understanding of our behavior, we have the potential to alleviate conflicts within ourselves, in our families, for organizations, and on a global scale.

I would like to express my immense appreciation to Neale Donald Walsch, whose wisdom and guidance were the catalysts for this work. Your encouragement and belief in my ability to contribute positively to the Israeli-Palestinian story were instrumental in the creation of this book. At the time I was already writing another book on the Dreem Leadership framework, Health, Head and Heart, which is based on the work that we deliver to CEOs and their teams, when you challenged me to put it to one side to take this on first.

I owe immense gratitude to my mentor and coach, Bob Proctor (may he rest in peace), whose wisdom empowered me to dream without constraints, regardless of external circumstances. Bob instilled in me the practice of being laser-like focused on my goals, the importance of inspired action, the courage to take leaps of faith, and the resilience to face the fear of rejection or criticism—especially in the pursuit of endeavors like writing this book. His most impactful lesson was teaching me how to keep my heart open amidst adversity and potential wrongdoings in life. This invaluable guidance provided me with the courage and conviction to write this book with both an open heart and a strong commitment to my values. Bob's voice and dedication will always be etched in my psyche.

I also extend a heartfelt thank you to Annette and Sam, whose generous hospitality at their home on the stunning shores of Sydney, Australia—where I reside—enabled me to craft the initial draft of this book. Nestled by the beach, surrounded by solitude, it was an idyllic setting, one of the most beautiful imaginable. Bundeena was an enchanting and deeply moving experience for me. As I sat by the shore, I was enveloped by an overwhelming sense of love and profound peace, knowing full well I was being guided and supported.

I owe a debt of gratitude to my family and friends for their unwavering support throughout this writing journey. Your encouragement, patience, and understanding during the countless hours spent writing and editing these pages have been invaluable.

To my large extended and beloved family living in Haifa and surrounding areas, your courage, love and commitment to growth and our people are a daily inspiration. Despite everything, you have been able to succeed, contribute and give back so much. I watch you from afar in awe and it gives me so much hope and determination to follow in your footsteps.

To my readers, followers, and the Dreem Coaching and Consulting community, your trust and enthusiasm for my work continue to inspire me. It is your commitment to personal and collective growth that fuels my passion for leadership and change. A lot of my courage comes from your continued encouragement and belief in our work. Without you, we would not be here.

I would also like to acknowledge the incredible team at Dreem Coaching and Consulting, who have been instrumental in turning my dream into a reality. Your dedication and commitment to our mission of meaningful growth have made this book possible. Thank you from the bottom of my heart.

I also want to express my gratitude to those who have shared their stories, experiences, and insights, which have enriched the narrative of *From the River to the Sea*. Your voices are a testament to the power of dialogue and empathy in resolving seemingly complex conflicts.

Lastly, I am deeply thankful for the opportunity to embark on this journey of self-discovery and collective change. The Israeli-Palestinian conflict is dubbed as being a complex and enduring one, but it is my hope that this book will simplify the picture, remove the noise, and focus on the root cause of the issue to help contribute to a future of greater understanding with true coexistence and harmony.

In closing, I want to reiterate that coexistence requires dismantling the borders and divisions that have plagued our world for far too long. Let us continue to challenge assumptions, embrace mindfulness, and take practical actions to unlock our full potential as individuals and as a global community.

Thank you all for your support, and I look forward to the positive impact *From the River to the Sea* may have on our collective journey towards a more peaceful and just world.

With gratitude and love,
Reem Borrows
Author | Speaker | Coach | Consultant
Dreem Coaching and Consulting

Thank You

If you have enjoyed or found value in this book, please take a moment to leave an honest/brief review on Amazon **amzn.to/3RuR3zD** or Goodreads. Your reviews help prospective readers decide if this is right for them & it is the greatest kindness you can offer the author.

Thank you in advance.

About the Author

Reem Borrows

Author | Speaker | Coach | Consultant

Reem Borrows is an accomplished author, speaker, coach, and consultant with a passion for seeking peace and justice for Palestinians and Jews in the Holy Land. She is the founder of Dreem Coaching and Consulting, a company dedicated to inspiring meaningful growth in individuals and companies.

With a career spanning over two decades, Reem has garnered extensive experience in developing high-level executives, teams, and individuals across various roles in the sales, marketing, and training domains. In 2020, she won the prestigious title of Australia's Best Corporate Trainer.

At Dreem Coaching and Consulting, Reem employs a holistic approach to leadership, managing business goals, and combining mindfulness with practical action to unlock the full potential of individuals.

Reem holds a Bachelor of Commerce degree, with a major in marketing, as well as a post-graduate diploma in Human Resource Management and Industrial Relations.

Work with Reem

As a seasoned leadership coach and consultant, Reem's commitment is to empower individuals, teams, and organizations to unlock their full potential. Through the Dreem Health, Head, and Heart Leadership framework, she guides people toward transformative personal and professional growth for results that stick. If you're looking for a partner in your leadership journey—one who combines expertise with genuine passion—she invites you to explore the possibilities of working together. You can contact her and the team at info@dreem.com.au, go to dreem.com.au and send us a message from there, or contact us on +61 1300437336.

Embark on a collaborative venture to enhance your leadership skills, foster organizational excellence, and achieve lasting success. Connect with her or the team to discuss how to tailor a coaching and consulting engagement that aligns seamlessly with your unique goals and aspirations. Your leadership evolution awaits; she and her team are there to champion your path to greatness, with balance, focus, and flow.

Also by Reem Borrows

SPARK: Women in the Business of Changing the World

About the Publisher

Red Thread Publishing is an all-female publishing company on a mission to support 10,000 women to become successful published authorpreneurs & thought leaders.

To work with us or connect regarding any of our growing library of books email us at **info@redthreadbooks.com.**

To learn more about us visit our website
www.redthreadbooks.com

Follow us & join the community.

facebook.com/redthreadpublishing
instagram.com/redthreadbooks

Other Red Thread Books

To see all our published works Visit Our Library:

bit.ly/RedThreadLibrary

Our books about writing & publishing:

The Anatomy of a Book: 21 Book Experts Share What Aspiring Authors Need to Know About Writing, Publishing & Book Marketing

Typo: The Art of Imperfect Creation, *Permission to do it badly*

Story Ink: *A cyclical Methodology to write 1 or 100 books*

Write: *An Interactive Guide to Drafting Your Manuscript*

~

Previous Collaborative Titles in the Brave New Voices Series:

Feisty: *Dangerously Amazing Women Using Their Voices & Making An Impact*

Spark: *Women in the Business of Changing the World - 1 sentence description*

Sanctuary: *Cultivating Safe Space in Sisterhood; Rediscovering the Power that Unites Us*

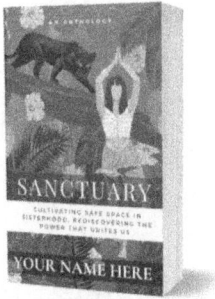

Sisterhood Redefines Us (Collaborative)

We are stronger together, but we must find or create our own safety first. (10 authors)

Dangerously Amazing Women (Collaborative)

If you're ready to rewrite all the rules & start thriving, just as you are, then Feisty is a must-read! (19 authors)

Women In the Business of Changing the World (Collaborative)

Celebrating the extraordinary impact of ordinary women, women when we show up & shine in our full, unapologetic authority. (10 authors)

Write & Publish with Us as a Collaborative Author

Be the next **Red Thread Collaborative Author**: bit.ly/46Yd6Ed

We believe every story matters, not just the stories of the women who can afford to publish them. Therefore we have built-in to our business structure scholarship funds using profits to support organizations for good in the world as well as our first-time authors anthology publishing.

∾

Access our Free Author Resources

bit.ly/RedThreadResources

Endnotes

Introduction

1. Authors unknown
2. Wikimedia Foundation. (2023, January 22). *Stolen generations.* Wikipedia. https://en.wikipedia.org/wiki/Stolen_Generations
3. Cosmic calendar. (n.d.) https://visav.phys.uvic.ca/~babul/AstroCourses/P303/BB-slide.htm
4. Doncaster, C. P. (n.d.). *Timeline of the human condition: Milestones in evolution and history.* https://www.southampton.ac.uk/~cpd/history.html

1. CHILD OF PEACE

1. Blackburn, N. (2021, May 16). *Jewish and Arab health professionals unite in Solidarity.* ISRAEL21c. https://www.israel21c.org/jewish-and-arab-health-professionals-unite-in-solidarity/
2. רמב"ם | הקריה הרפואית לבריאות האד (May 18 2021). *News and events.* Rambam Health Care Campus. https://www.rambam.org.il/en/rambam_news/we_are_together.aspx
3. *Counting the Dead: Estimating the Loss of Life in the Indigenous ...* (n.d.). https://www.se.edu/native-american/wp-content/uploads/sites/49/2019/09/A-NAS-2017-Proceedings-Smith.pdf

2. THE AWAKENING

1. United Nations High Commissioner for Refugees. (n.d.). *Global Trends.* UNHCR. https://www.unhcr.org/globaltrends.html
2. Taibbi, M. (2019, March 22). *16 Years Later, How the Press that Sold the Iraq War Got Away With It.* Rolling Stone. https://www.rollingstone.com/politics/politics-features/iraq-war-media-fail-matt-taibbi-812230/
3. King, K. C. (2022, January 28). *The Domino Effect: Impact Reflection.* North Berkeley Wealth Management. Retrieved February 21, 2023, from https://northberkeleywealth.com/articles/the-domino-effect

3. THE STORY

1. Staff, A. J. (2021, May 16). *'Give US 10 Minutes': How Israel Bombed a Gaza Media Tower.* Gaza News | Al Jazeera. Retrieved March 6, 2023, from https://www.aljazeera.com/news/2021/5/15/give-us-10-minutes-how-israel-bombed-gaza-media-tower

2. ABC News Network. (n.d.). ABC News. https://abcnews.go.com/International/israeli-strike-kills-boys-playing-gaza-beach/story?id=24583817

3. Guardian News and Media. (2013, May 23). *Father of Muhammad al-Dura Rebukes Israeli Report on Son's Death.* The Guardian. https://www.theguardian.com/world/2013/may/23/israeli-report-denies-death-al-dura

4. *Who Are Jews? An Overview of Jewish History From Ancient Times On, and the Origins of Antisemitism.* UW Stroum Center for Jewish Studies. (2022, October 3). https://jewishstudies.washington.edu/who-are-jews-jewish-history-origins-antisemitism

    Romans destroy and Plow Jerusalem. 135 AD. (n.d.). http://www.about-bibleprophecy.com/e31.htm

5. Encyclopædia Britannica, inc. (n.d.). *Theodor Herzl.* Encyclopædia Britannica. https://www.britannica.com/biography/Theodor-Herzl

6. *Digital Maps of Jewish Populations in Europe (1750 – 1950) for online ...* (n.d.). https://www.iijg.org/wp-content/uploads/2018/01/LeitenbergCrystall-Jewish-PopulationsMaps-Report-updated.pdf

7. Staff, C. I. E. (2022, April 20). *Napoleon Issues Proclamation Which Calls Jews Rightful Heirs of Palestine.* CIE. Retrieved January 24, 2023, from https://israeled.org/napoleon-issues-proclamation-calls-jews-rightful-heirs-palestine/

8. *Genocide.* Genocide - An Overview | ScienceDirect Topics. (n.d.). https://www.sciencedirect.com/topics/medicine-and-dentistry/genocide

9. Tahhan, Z. A. (2018, November 2). *More Than a Century On: The Balfour Declaration Explained.* Features | Al Jazeera. https://www.aljazeera.com/features/2018/11/2/more-than-a-century-on-the-balfour-declaration-explained

10. *The Forgotten Truth About the Balfour Declaration - Harvard University.* (n.d.). https://scholar.harvard.edu/files/martinkramer/files/forgotten_truth_balfour_declaration.pdf

11. *Jewish & Non-Jewish Population of Israel/Palestine.* (1517-Present). (n.d.). https://www.jewishvirtuallibrary.org/jewish-and-non-jewish-population-of-israel-palestine-1517-present

4. THE TRUTH

1. Walsch, Neale Donald. *What God Wants.* Hodder Mobius, 2005.

5. THE REALITY

1. Michal. (2017, June 22). *The Holocaust: The National WWII Museum: New Orleans*. https://www.nationalww2museum.org/war/articles/holocaust
2. Wikimedia Foundation. (2023, January 1). *World War II Casualties*. Wikipedia. https://en.wikipedia.org/wiki/World_War_II_casualties
3. *July 22: A Pivotal Day in Terrorism History*. War on the Rocks. (2021, July 22). https://warontherocks.com/2021/07/july-22-a-pivotal-day-in-terrorism-history/

6. THE CATASTROPHE (NAKBA)

1. Haddad, M. (2022, May 15). *Nakba Day: What Happened in Palestine in 1948?* Israel-Palestine conflict News | Al Jazeera.https://www.aljazeera.com/news/2022/5/15/nakba-mapping-palestinian-villages-destroyed-by-israel-in-1948
   Ufheil-Somers, A. (2016, September 2). *Gaza as an Open-Air Prison*. MERIP. https://merip.org/2015/06/gaza-as-an-open-air-prison/#:~:text=Prime%20Minister%20David%20Cameron%20of,and%20out%20of%20the%20Strip.
2. Al Jazeera. (2017, May 23). *The Nakba Did Not Start or End in 1948*. Features | Al Jazeera.https://www.aljazeera.com/features/2017/5/23/the-nakba-did-not-start-or-end-in-1948
3. Haddad, M. (2022, May 15). *Nakba Day: What Happened in Palestine in 1948?* Israel-Palestine conflict News | Al Jazeera.https://www.aljazeera.com/news/2022/5/15/nakba-mapping-palestinian-villages-destroyed-by-israel-in-1948
4. United Nations. (n.d.). *Universal Declaration of Human Rights*. United Nations. https://www.un.org/en/about-us/universal-declaration-of-human-rights
5. BBC. (2012, October 17). *Israel Forced to Release Study on Gaza Blockade*. BBC https://www.bbc.com/news/world-middle-east-19975211
6. *The Occupation of Water*. Amnesty International. (2022, August 5). https://www.amnesty.org/en/latest/campaigns/2017/11/the-occupation-of-water/
   50 Stories of Palestinian Life Under Occupation. (n.d.). https://www.ochaopt.org/50Stories/
   What are the Issues Facing Palestinians Today? (n.d.). https://www.map.org.uk/the-issues/the-issues
7. Shakir, O. (2022, October 27). *A Threshold Crossed*. Human Rights Watch. Retrieved https://www.hrw.org/report/2021/04/27/threshold-crossed/israeli-authorities-and-crimes-apartheid-and-persecution
   Data on Demolition and Displacement in the West Bank. United Nations Office for the Coordination of Humanitarian Affairs - occupied Palestinian territory. (n.d.). https://www.ochaopt.org/data/demolition

8. *The Occupied Territories and International Law | b'tselem.* (n.d.). https://www.bt-selem.org/international_law

9. *The Discriminatory Laws Database.* Adalah. (n.d.). https://www.adalah.org/en/content/view/7771

10. *Israel: Discriminatory Land Policies Hem in Palestinians.* Human Rights Watch. (2020, October 28).

11. Cohen, N. W. (2003). *The Americanization of Zionism, 1897-1948.* Brandeis University Press, published by University Press of New England.

10. THE SOLUTION

1. Incidentally, Aunt Khazni would make the same gestures about the man I should one day marry. She would always say, "Reem, make sure you marry a man who is generous with his time and money – Kareem," as she opened her palm gently, "and not tight – Bakheel," as she clenched her palm tightly shut, "Otherwise, life will be tough on you."

11. THE CHOICE

1. Spetalnick, M. (2016, September 14). *U.S., Israel Sign $38 billion Military Aid Package.* Reuters. https://www.reuters.com/article/us-usa-israel-statement-idUSKCN11K2CI

2. Wikimedia Foundation. (2023, January 26). *Jewish Population By Country.* Wikipedia. https://en.wikipedia.org/wiki/Jewish_population_by_country

3. Arab Center Washington DC. (2022, January 3). *Brief Report on the Population of Palestine at the End of 2021.* Arab Center Washington DC. https://arabcenter-dc.org/resource/brief-report-on-the-population-of-palestine-at-the-end-of-2021/

4. *Adapted from Neale Donald Walsch's - The Mechanics of the Mind Training Video*

5. Wahat al-Salam - Neve Shalom. (2022, November 8). *Community.* https://wasns.org/-community-/

12. THE CHANGE

1. Hill, N., & Ramsey, D. (2022). *Think and Grow Rich.* Ramsey Press.

2. Blackburn, N. (2016, October 31). *The Small Israeli Village Where Everyone's a Doctor.* ISRAEL21c. https://www.israel21c.org/the-small-israeli-village-where-everyones-a-doctor/

3. YOURDICTIONARY. (n.d.). *Famous Examples of Civil Disobedience in History.* YourDictionary. https://examples.yourdictionary.com/famous-examples-of-civil-disobedience-in-history.html

4. Adalah: An Independent Human Rights Organization and Legal Center That Promotes and Defends the Rights of Palestinian Arab Citizens of Israel.

American Task Force on Palestine (ATFP): Advocates for a negotiated agreement that provides for two states living side by side in peace and security.

Arik Institute: Fosters reconciliation, tolerance, and peace between Israelis and Palestinians.

Bat Shalom: A feminist grassroots organization of Jewish and Palestinian Israeli women working together towards peace and a just resolution to the conflict.

Breaking the Silence: An organization of veteran combatants who expose the reality of everyday life in the Occupied Territories.

B'Tselem: Documents and educates the public to combat human rights violations in the Occupied Territories.

Encounter: Transforms the Israeli-Palestinian conflict and heals internal Jewish communal rifts through educating Jewish leaders about Palestinian life.

Palestinian Federation of Chile: Strengthens cultural ties between Palestine and Chile.

Irish Palestine Solidarity Campaign: Promotes solidarity between Ireland and Palestine .

Al Haq: A Palestinian non-governmental human rights organization that documents and advocates for human rights violations in Israel and Palestine.

Al-Mezan: A Palestinian human rights organization that offers legal support to victims of human rights violations.

The Freedom Theatre: A cultural, artistic, and media organization that advances freedom and social justice through creative means of public education.

APAN: The Australian Palestinian Advocacy Network is a national coalition harnessing the passion of Australians for Palestinian human rights, justice, and equality.

Jewish Voice for Peace: Is a national organization dedicated to a U.S. foreign policy based on peace, human rights, and respect for international law.

www.ingramcontent.com/pod-product-compliance
Lightning Source LLC
Chambersburg PA
CBHW022052020426
42335CB00012B/659